UML Distilled
Second Edition

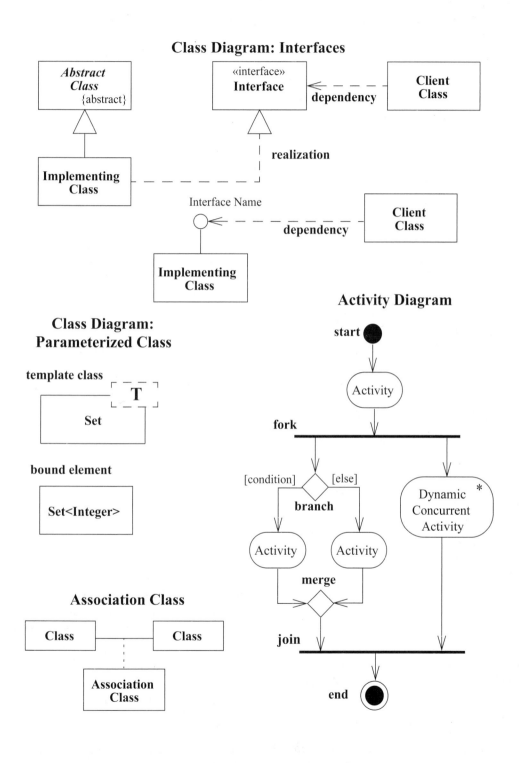

Class Diagram: Interfaces

Abstract
Class
{abstract}

«interface»
Interface

Client
Class

dependency

Implementing
Class

realization

Interface Name

Implementing
Class

dependency

Client
Class

Class Diagram:
Parameterized Class

template class

T

Set

bound element

Set<Integer>

Association Class

Class | Class

Association
Class

Activity Diagram

start

Activity

fork

[condition]   [else]

branch

Activity   Activity

merge

join

Dynamic
Concurrent
Activity *

end

The Addison-Wesley Object Technology Series

Grady Booch, Ivar Jacobson, and James Rumbaugh, Series Editors
For more information, check out the series Web site [http://www.awprofessional.com/otseries/].

Ahmed/Umrysh, *Developing Enterprise Java Applications with J2EE™ and UML*

Arlow/Neustadt, *UML and the Unified Process: Practical Object-Oriented Analysis and Design*

Armour/Miller, *Advanced Use Case Modeling: Software Systems*

Bellin/Simone, *The CRC Card Book*

Binder, *Testing Object-Oriented Systems: Models, Patterns, and Tools*

Bittner/Spence, *Use Case Modeling*

Blakley, *CORBA Security: An Introduction to Safe Computing with Objects*

Booch, *Object Solutions: Managing the Object-Oriented Project*

Booch, *Object-Oriented Analysis and Design with Applications, Second Edition*

Booch/Bryan, *Software Engineering with ADA, Third Edition*

Booch/Rumbaugh/Jacobson, *The Unified Modeling Language User Guide*

Box/Brown/Ewald/Sells, *Effective COM: 50 Ways to Improve Your COM and MTS-based Applications*

Carlson, *Modeling XML Applications with UML: Practical e-Business Applications*

Cockburn, *Surviving Object-Oriented Projects: A Manager's Guide*

Collins, *Designing Object-Oriented User Interfaces*

Conallen, *Building Web Applications with UML, Second Edition*

D'Souza/Wills, *Objects, Components, and Frameworks with UML: The Catalysis Approach*

Douglass, *Doing Hard Time: Developing Real-Time Systems with UML, Objects, Frameworks, and Patterns*

Douglass, *Real-Time Design Patterns: Robust Scalable Architecture for Real-Time Systems*

Douglass, *Real-Time UML, Second Edition: Developing Efficient Objects for Embedded Systems*

Eeles/Houston/Kozaczynski, *Building J2EE™ Applications with the Rational Unified Process*

Fontoura/Pree/Rumpe, *The UML Profile for Framework Architectures*

Fowler, *Analysis Patterns: Reusable Object Models*

Fowler/Beck/Brant/Opdyke/Roberts, *Refactoring: Improving the Design of Existing Code*

Fowler/Scott, *UML Distilled, Second Edition: A Brief Guide to the Standard Object Modeling Language*

Gomaa, *Designing Concurrent, Distributed, and Real-Time Applications with UML*

Graham, *Object-Oriented Methods, Third Edition: Principles and Practice*

Heinckiens, *Building Scalable Database Applications: Object-Oriented Design, Architectures, and Implementations*

Hofmeister/Nord/Dilip, *Applied Software Architecture*

Jacobson/Booch/Rumbaugh, *The Unified Software Development Process*

Jordan, *C++ Object Databases: Programming with the ODMG Standard*

Kruchten, *The Rational Unified Process, An Introduction, Second Edition*

Lau, *The Art of Objects: Object-Oriented Design and Architecture*

Leffingwell/Widrig, *Managing Software Requirements: A Unified Approach*

Marshall, *Enterprise Modeling with UML: Designing Successful Software through Business Analysis*

McGregor/Sykes, *A Practical Guide to Testing Object-Oriented Software*

Mellor/Balcer, *Executable UML: A Foundation for Model-Driven Architecture*

Mowbray/Ruh, *Inside CORBA: Distributed Object Standards and Applications*

Naiburg/Maksimchuk, *UML for Database Design*

Oestereich, *Developing Software with UML: Object-Oriented Analysis and Design in Practice, Second Edition*

Page-Jones, *Fundamentals of Object-Oriented Design in UML*

Pohl, *Object-Oriented Programming Using C++, Second Edition*

Quatrani, *Visual Modeling with Rational Rose 2002 and UML*

Rector/Sells, *ATL Internals*

Reed, *Developing Applications with Visual Basic and UML*

Rosenberg/Scott, *Applying Use Case Driven Object Modeling with UML: An Annotated e-Commerce Example*

Rosenberg/Scott, *Use Case Driven Object Modeling with UML: A Practical Approach*

Royce, *Software Project Management: A Unified Framework*

Rumbaugh/Jacobson/Booch, *The Unified Modeling Language Reference Manual*

Schneider/Winters, *Applying Use Cases, Second Edition: A Practical Guide*

Shan/Earle, *Enterprise Computing with Objects: From Client/Server Environments to the Internet*

Smith/Williams, *Performance Solutions: A Practical Guide to Creating Responsive, Scalable Software*

Stevens/Pooley, *Using UML, Updated Edition: Software Engineering with Objects and Components*

Unhelkar, *Process Quality Assurance for UML-Based Projects*

van Harmelen, *Object Modeling and User Interface Design: Designing Interactive Systems*

Warmer/Kleppe, *The Object Constraint Language: Precise Modeling with UML*

White, *Software Configuration Management Strategies and Rational ClearCase®: A Practical Introduction*

The Component Software Series

Clemens Szyperski, Series Editor
For more information, check out the series Web site [http://www.awprofessional.com/csseries/].

Allen, *Realizing eBusiness with Components*

Atkinson/Bayer/Bunse/Kamsties/Laitenberger/Laqua/Muthig/Paech/Wust/Zettel, *Component-Based Product Line Engineering with UML*

Cheesman/Daniels, *UML Components: A Simple Process for Specifying Component-Based Software*

Szyperski, *Component Software, Second Edition: Beyond Object-Oriented Programming*

Whitehead, *Component-Based Development: Principles and Planning for Business Systems*

UML Distilled
Second Edition

A Brief Guide to the Standard Object Modeling Language

Martin Fowler

with

Kendall Scott

ADDISON–WESLEY

Boston • San Francisco • New York • Toronto • Montreal
London • Munich • Paris • Madrid
Capetown • Sydney • Tokyo • Singapore • Mexico City

Many of the designations used by manufacturers and sellers to distinguish their products are claimed as trademarks. Where those designations appear in this book, and Addison Wesley Longman, Inc., was aware of a trademark claim, the designations have been printed in initial capital letters or all capital letters.

The author and publisher have taken care in preparation of this book, but make no express or implied warranty of any kind and assume no responsibility for errors or omissions. No liability is assumed for incidental or consequential damages in connection with or arising out of the use of the information or programs contained herein.

The publisher offers discounts on this book when ordered in quantity for special sales. For more information, please contact: Pearson Education Corporate Sales Division; 201 W. 103rd Street; Indianapolis, IN 46290; (800) 428-5331; corpsales@pearsoned.com

Library of Congress Cataloging-in-Publication Data

Fowler, Martin.
    UML distilled: a brief guide to the standard object modeling language / Martin Fowler with Kendall Scott. — 2nd ed.
        p.   cm. — (Object technology series)
    Includes biographical references and index.
    ISBN 0-201-65783-X (alk. paper)
    1. Object-oriented methods (Computer science) 2. Computer software—development. 3. UML (Computer science)   I. Scott, Kendall.   II. Title.   III. Series.
    QA76.9.035F694   1999
    005.1'2—dc21
                                                                    99-33476
                                                                        CIP

Copyright © 2000 by Addison Wesley Longman, Inc.

Executive Editor: J. Carter Shanklin
Assistant Editor: Krysia Bebick
Project Manager: Sarah Weaver
Copyeditor: Evelyn Pyle
Proofreader: Maine Proofreading Services
Index and Composition: Kendall Scott
Cover Design: Simone Payment

Text printed on recycled and acid-free paper.

ISBN   020165783X

11 1213141516 CRS   05 04 03 02

11th Printing   November 2002

Contents

Figures

Foreword

When we began to craft the Unified Modeling Language, we hoped that we could produce a standard means of expressing design that would not only reflect the best practices of industry, but would also help demystify the process of software system modeling. We believed that the availability of a standard modeling language would encourage more developers to model their software systems before building them. The rapid and widespread adoption of the UML demonstrates that the benefits of modeling are indeed well known to the developer community.

The creation of the UML was itself an iterative and incremental process very similar to the modeling of a large software system. The end result is a standard built on, and reflective of, the many ideas and contributions made by numerous individuals and companies from the object community. We began the UML effort, but many others helped bring it to a successful conclusion; we are grateful for their contribution.

Creating and agreeing on a standard modeling language is a significant challenge by itself. Educating the development community, and presenting the UML in a manner that is both accessible and in the con-text of the software development process, is also a significant challenge. In this deceptively short book, updated to reflect the most recent changes to the UML, Martin Fowler has more than met this challenge.

In a clear and friendly style, Martin not only introduces the key aspects of UML, but also clearly demonstrates the role UML plays in the development process. Along the way, we are treated to abundant nuggets of modeling insight and wisdom drawn from Martin's 12-plus years of design and modeling experience.

The result is a book that has introduced many thousands of developers to UML, whetting their appetite to further explore the many benefits of modeling with this now standard modeling language.

We recommend the book to any modeler or developer interested in getting a first look at UML and in gaining a perspective on the key role it plays in the development process.

Grady Booch
Ivar Jacobson
James Rumbaugh

Preface

Two years ago, Addison-Wesley approached me to write a book about the then-new UML. At that time, there was a lot of interest in the UML, but only a standards document from which to learn about it. We broke many records to quickly produce a short introductory guide to the new UML, something that would provide some guidance until the more detailed and official books were to appear later that year.

We didn't expect this book to last after more detailed books appeared. Most people believed that given the choice between a slim overview and a detailed text, everyone would pick the detailed text. Although that was the general view, I believed that even in the presence of detailed books, there was still room for a concise summary.

Two years later, my hopes have been realized more than I could have wished. *UML Distilled* has been, in computer industry terms, a best-seller. Even though good detailed books have appeared on the UML, the book still sells well. Better than that, more slim books have appeared, confirming my belief that in a world with so much information, there is value in well-chosen brevity.

Now, that's all very well, but should you buy this book?

I'm going to assume you've heard about the UML. It has become the standard way to draw diagrams of object-oriented designs, and it has also spread into non-OO fields. The major pre-UML methods have all died out. The UML has arrived and is here to stay.

If you want to learn about the UML, this book is one way to do it. The main reason for starting with this book is that it's a *small* book. Buying a big book will give you more information, but it will also take you longer to read. I've selected the most important parts of the UML so that you don't have to. With this book, you'll pick up the key elements of the notation and what they mean. If you want to move further, you can move to a more detailed book later.

If you want a longer tutorial to the UML, I suggest the *Unified Modeling Language User Guide* (Booch, Rumbaugh, and Jacobson 1999). The *User Guide* is able to cover a lot more ground. It's well written and organized in a way that explains how to apply the UML to various modeling problems.

Both this book and the *User Guide* assume that you know something about OO development. Although many people have told me that this book is a good introduction to objects, I didn't write it with that in mind. If you're looking for an introduction to objects with the UML, you should also consider Craig Larman's book (Larman 1998).

Although the main point of this book is the UML, I've also added material that complements the UML material. The UML is a relatively small part of what you need to know to succeed with objects, and I think that it's important to point out some of the other things here.

The most important of these is software process. The UML is designed to be independent of process. You can do anything you like; all the UML does is say what your diagrams mean. However, the diagrams don't make much sense without a process to give them context. I also believe that process is important and that a good process doesn't need to be complicated.

So, I've described a lightweight outline process for OO software development. This provides a context for the techniques and will help to get you going in using objects.

The other topics include patterns, refactoring, self-testing code, design by contract, and CRC cards. None of these are part of the UML, yet they are valuable techniques that I use regularly.

Structure of the Book

Chapter 1 looks at what the UML is, the history of its development, and the reasons why you might want to use it.

Chapter 2 discusses the object-oriented development process. Although the UML exists independent of process, I find it hard to discuss modeling techniques without talking about where they fit in with object-oriented development.

Chapters 3 through 6 discuss the three most important techniques in the UML: use cases, class diagrams, and interaction models. The UML is a large beast, but you don't need all of it. These three techniques are the core that almost everyone needs. Start with these and add the others as you need them. (Note that since class diagrams are so complicated in themselves, I've put the key parts of class diagrams in Chapter 4 and the advanced concepts in Chapter 6.)

Chapters 7 through 10 explore the remaining techniques. All of these are valuable, but not every project needs every technique. So these chapters provide enough information to tell you what the technique is and whether you need it.

For all of these techniques, I describe the notation, explain what the notation means, and provide tips about using the techniques. My philosophy is to make clear what the UML says and, at the same time, to give you my opinions on how best to use it. I've also added pointers to other books that provide more detail.

Chapter 11 gives a small example to show how the UML fits in with programming using (of course) Java.

The inside covers summarize the UML notation. You may find it useful to refer to these as you are reading the chapters so that you can check on the notation for the various modeling concepts.

If you find this book interesting, you can find other information on my work related to using the UML, patterns, and refactoring at my home page (see page xix).

Changes for the Second Edition

As the UML evolved, and I received feedback about the first edition of the book, I continually updated it. We reprinted every two or three months; nearly every printing contained updates, which resulted in considerable strain on the processes of the publishing industry.

With the change from UML 1.2 to 1.3, we decided to do a more thorough overhaul of the book, enough to produce a second edition. Since the book has been so popular, I've tried not to change the essential spirit of the book. I've carefully tried to not add much, and to see whether there are things I can take away.

The biggest changes are in Chapter 3, about use cases, and Chapter 9, about activity diagrams, which have each received a severe rewrite. I've also added a section on collaborations to Chapter 7. Elsewhere, I've taken the opportunity to make a host of smaller changes, based on feedback and my experiences over the last couple of years.

Acknowledgments for the First Edition

Putting out a book this fast required a lot of help from people who went beyond the normal effort that goes into producing a book to do everything that much more quickly.

Kendall Scott played an important role in pulling together all the material and working over the text and graphics. As I've revised the book, he has continued to keep everything in shape, conquering a series of tasks that came with little notice and impossible deadlines.

The three amigos, Grady Booch, Ivar Jacobson, and Jim Rumbaugh, have been full of support and advice. We have burned up many hours of transcontinental phone calls, and they have improved the book greatly (as well as my understanding of the UML).

A good slate of book reviewers is essential to doing a good job on a book. Not only did these reviewers give me the feedback I needed, they also turned around their comments in less than a week to keep to our tight deadlines. My thanks to: Simmi Kochhar Bhargava of Netscape Communications Corporation, Eric Evans, Tom Hadfield of Evolve Software, Inc., Ronald E. Jeffries, Joshua Kerievsky of Industrial Logic, Inc., Helen Klein of the University of Michigan, James Odell, and Vivek Salgar of Netscape Communications Corporation. Double thanks to Tom Hadfield because he did it twice!

I want to thank Jim Odell for two things: first, for coordinating the Object Management Group (OMG) effort to get a single standard UML, which will be a big step forward for our industry; and second, for encouraging me to get into the object-oriented analysis and design field. Oh, and thanks for reviewing the book, too!

Thanks to Cindy for dealing with me being absent even when I was home.

I can't even imagine the difficulties that my editor, J. Carter Shanklin, and his assistant, Angela Buenning, went through to get this book out as quickly as they did. Whatever these difficulties were, I'm sure Carter and Angela deserve my thanks. The book industry is not designed to cope with changing a book every couple of months, but Carter and his team have done a good job of hiding that fact!

In keeping this book up to date, I've often had questions about specific details in the UML. Conrad Bock, Ivar Jacobson, Cris Kobryn, Jim Odell, Guus Ramackers, and Jim Rumbaugh have all gone out of their way to help me find these answers.

Numerous people have sent me messages pointing out various errors and omissions; there are too many to list here, I'm afraid, but I thank you all.

Last, but not least, thanks to my parents for helping me start off with a good education, from which all else springs.

Martin Fowler
Melrose, Massachusetts
April 1999
fowler@acm.org
http://ourworld.compuserve.com/homepages/Martin_Fowler

Chapter 1

Introduction

What Is the UML?

The **Unified Modeling Language (UML)** is the successor to the wave of object-oriented analysis and design (OOA&D) methods that appeared in the late '80s and early '90s. It most directly unifies the methods of Booch, Rumbaugh (OMT), and Jacobson, but its reach is wider than that. The UML went through a standardization process with the OMG (Object Management Group) and is now an OMG standard.

The UML is called a modeling language, not a method. Most methods consist, at least in principle, of both a modeling language and a process. The **modeling language** is the (mainly graphical) notation that methods use to express designs. The **process** is their advice on what steps to take in doing a design.

The process parts of many methods books are rather sketchy. Furthermore, I find that most people, when they say they are using a method, use the modeling language, but rarely follow the process. So in many ways, the modeling language is the most important part of the method. It is certainly the key part for communication. If you want to discuss your design with someone, it is the modeling language that both of you need to understand, *not* the process you used to get to that design.

The three amigos have also developed a unified process, which they call the Rational Unified Process (RUP). You don't have to use the Rational Unified Process in order to use the UML—they are distinctly separate. In this book, however, I talk a little bit about process in order to put the techniques of the modeling language in context. Within this discussion, I use the basic steps and terms of the Rational Unified Process, but the text is *not* a description of the Rational Unified Process. I find that I use many different processes, depending on my client and on the kind of software I am building. Although I think that a standard modeling language is valuable, I don't see a comparable need for a standard process, although some harmonization on vocabulary would be useful.

How We Got Here

In the 1980s, objects began to move away from the research labs and took their first steps toward the "real" world. Smalltalk stabilized into a platform that people could use, and C++ was born.

Like many developments in software, objects were driven by programming languages. Many people wondered how design methods would fit into an object-oriented world. Design methods had become very popular in industrial development in the '70s and '80s. Many felt that techniques to help people do good analysis and design were just as important to object-oriented development.

The key books about object-oriented analysis and design methods appeared between 1988 and 1992:

- Sally Shlaer and Steve Mellor wrote a pair of books (1989 and 1991) on analysis and design; the material in these books has evolved into their Recursive Design approach (1997).

- Peter Coad and Ed Yourdon also wrote books that developed Coad's lightweight and prototype-oriented approach to methods. See Coad and Yourdon (1991a and 1991b), Coad and Nicola (1993), and Coad *et al.* (1995).

- The Smalltalk community in Portland, Oregon, came up with Responsibility-Driven Design (Wirfs-Brock *et al.* 1990) and Class-Responsibility-Collaboration (CRC) cards (Beck and Cunningham 1989).

- Grady Booch had done a lot of work with Rational Software in developing Ada systems. His books featured several examples (and the best cartoons in the world of methods books). See Booch (1994 and 1996).

- Jim Rumbaugh led a team at the research labs at General Electric, which came out with a very popular book about a method called Object Modeling Technique (OMT). See Rumbaugh *et al.* (1991) and Rumbaugh (1996).

- Jim Odell based his books (written with James Martin) on his long experience with business information systems and Information Engineering. The result was the most conceptual of these books. See Martin and Odell (1994).

- Ivar Jacobson built his books on his experience with telephone switches for Ericsson and introduced the concept of use cases in the first one. See Jacobson (1992 and 1995).

As I prepared to travel to Portland for the OOPSLA conference in 1994, the methods scene was pretty split and competitive. Each of the aforementioned authors was now informally leading a group of practitioners who liked his ideas. All of these methods were very similar, yet they contained a number of often annoying minor differences among them. The same basic concepts would appear in very different notations, which caused confusion to my clients.

Talk of standardization had surfaced, but nobody seemed willing to do anything about it. Some were opposed to the very idea of standards for methods. Others liked the idea but were not willing to put in any effort. A team from the OMG tried to look at standardization but got only an open letter of protest from all the key methodologists. Grady Booch tried an informal morning coffee approach, with no more success. (This reminds me of an old joke. Question: What is the difference between a methodologist and a terrorist? Answer: You can negotiate with a terrorist.)

For the OO methods community, the big news at OOPSLA '94 was that Jim Rumbaugh had left General Electric to join Grady Booch at Rational Software, with the intention of merging their methods.

The next year was full of amusements.

Grady and Jim proclaimed that "the methods war is over—we won," basically declaring that they were going to achieve standardization the Microsoft way. A number of other methodologists suggested forming an Anti-Booch Coalition.

By OOPSLA '95, Grady and Jim had prepared their first public description of their merged method: version 0.8 of the *Unified Method* documentation. Even more significantly, they announced that Rational Software had bought Objectory, and that Ivar Jacobson would be joining the Unified team. Rational held a party to celebrate the release of the 0.8 draft that was very well attended. It was also quite a lot of fun, despite Jim Rumbaugh's singing.

During 1996, Grady, Jim, and Ivar, now widely referred to as the three amigos, worked on their method, under its new name: the Unified Modeling Language (UML). However, the other major players in the object methods community were not inclined to let the UML be the last word.

An OMG task force was formed to do standardization in the methods area. This represented a much more serious attempt to address the issues than previous OMG efforts in the methods area. Mary Loomis was given the chair; later Jim Odell joined as co-chair and took over leadership of the effort. Odell made it clear that he was prepared to give up his method to a standard, but he did not want a Rational-imposed standard.

In January 1997, various organizations submitted proposals for a methods standard to facilitate the interchange of models. These proposals focus on a metamodel and an optional notation. Rational released version 1.0 of the UML documentation as their proposal to the OMG.

There then followed a short period of arm-twisting while the various proposals were merged. The OMG adopted the resulting 1.1 as an official OMG standard. Since then, a Revision Task Force (RTF), led by Cris Kobryn, made some incremental revisions. Version 1.2 was cosmetic, but version 1.3, made public in early 1999, had more significance. The RTF expects to complete its work in the spring of 1999, releasing version 1.3 as the next official version of the UML.

Notations and Metamodels

The UML, in its current state, defines a notation and a metamodel.

The **notation** is the graphical stuff you see in models; it is the syntax of the modeling language. For instance, class diagram notation defines how items and concepts such as class, association, and multiplicity are represented.

Of course, this leads to the question of what exactly is meant by an association or multiplicity or even a class. Common usage suggests some informal definitions, but many people want more rigor than that.

The idea of rigorous specification and design languages is most prevalent in the field of formal methods. In such techniques, designs and specifications are represented using some derivative of predicate calculus. Such definitions are mathematically rigorous and allow no ambiguity. However, the value of these definitions is by no means universal. Even if you can prove that a program satisfies a mathematical specification, there is no way to prove that the mathematical specification actually meets the real requirements of the system.

Design is all about seeing the key issues in the development. Formal methods often lead to getting bogged down in lots of minor details. Also, formal methods are hard to understand and manipulate, often harder to deal with than programming languages. And you can't even execute them.

Most OO methods have very little rigor; their notation appeals to intuition rather than formal definition. On the whole, this does not seem to have done much harm. These methods may be informal, but many people still find them useful—and it is usefulness that counts.

However, OO methods people are looking for ways to improve the rigor of methods without sacrificing their usefulness. One way to do this is to define a **metamodel:** a diagram, usually a class diagram, that defines the notation.

Figure 1-1 is a small piece of the UML metamodel that shows the relationship among features. (The extract is there just to give you a flavor of what metamodels are like. I'm not even going to try to explain it.)

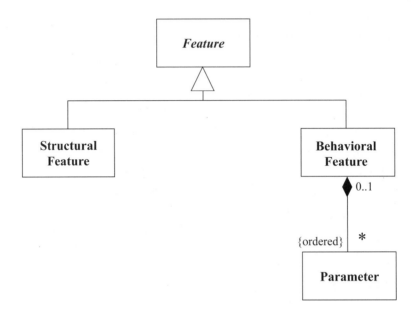

Figure 1-1: *UML Metamodel Extract*

How much does the metamodel affect the user of the modeling notation? Well, it does help define what is a well-formed model—that is, one that is syntactically correct. As such, a methods power user should understand the metamodel. However, most users of methods do not need such understanding to get some value out of using the UML notation.

I am not rigorous in this book; rather, I follow the traditional methods path and appeal to your intuition. If you want greater rigor, you should peruse the reference manual or the official documentation.

How strictly should you stick to the modeling language? That depends on the purpose for which you are using it. If you have a CASE tool that generates code, you have to stick to the CASE tool's interpretation of the modeling language in order to get acceptable code. If you are using the diagrams for communication purposes, you have a little more leeway.

If you stray from the official notation, other developers will not fully understand what you are saying. However, there are times when the official notation can get in the way of your needs. I'll admit that in these cases, I'm not at all afraid to bend the language. I believe that the language should bend to help me communicate, rather than the other way around. But I don't do it often, and I'm always aware that a bend is a bad thing if it causes communication problems. In this book, I mention those places where I'm inclined to do a bit of bending.

Why Do Analysis and Design?

When it comes down to it, the real point of software development is cutting code. Diagrams are, after all, just pretty pictures. No user is going to thank you for pretty pictures; what a user wants is software that executes.

So when you are considering using the UML, it is important to ask yourself why you are doing it and how it will help you when it comes down to writing the code. There's no proper empirical evidence to prove that these techniques are good or bad, but the following subsections discuss the reasons that I often come across for using them.

In this section, I talk a little about techniques that I'll discuss later. If you find these forward references confusing, just skip this section and come back to it later.

Communication

The fundamental reason to use the UML involves communication. I use the UML because it allows me to communicate certain concepts more clearly than the alternatives. Natural language is too imprecise and gets tangled when it comes to more complex concepts. Code is precise but too detailed. So I use the UML when I want a certain amount of precision but I don't want to get lost in details. That doesn't mean I avoid details; rather, I use the UML to highlight *important* details.

As a consultant, I often have to breeze into a complex project and look intelligent in a very short period of time. I find the UML invaluable for that because it helps me acquire an overall view of the system. A look at a class diagram can quickly tell me what kinds of abstractions are present in the system and where the questionable parts are that need further work. As I probe deeper, I want to see how classes collaborate, so I ask to see interaction diagrams that illustrate key behaviors in the system.

If this is useful to me as an outsider, it is just as useful to the regular project team. It's easy to lose sight of the forest for the trees on a large project. With a few choice diagrams in hand, you can find your way around the software much more easily.

To build a road map of a large system, use package diagrams (see Chapter 7) to show the major parts of a system and their interdependencies. For each package, you can then draw a class diagram. When you draw a class diagram in this context, take a specification perspective. It is very important to hide implementations with this kind of work. You should also draw interaction diagrams for the key interactions in the package.

Use patterns (see page 33) to describe the important ideas in the system that appear in multiple places. Patterns help you to explain why your design is the way it is. It is also useful to describe designs you have rejected and why you rejected them. I always end up forgetting that kind of decision.

When you follow these guidelines, keep the results brief. An important part of communication is in highlighting the important things to say. You don't have to show every feature of every class; you should instead show the important details. A brief document communicates much better than a thick one; the art is knowing what to leave out.

Learning OO

A lot of people talk about the learning curve associated with OO—the infamous paradigm shift. In some ways, the switch to OO is easy. In other ways, there are a number of obstacles to working with objects, particularly in using them to their best advantage.

It's not that it's difficult to learn how to program in an OO language. The problem is that it takes a while to learn to exploit the advantages that object languages provide. Tom Hadfield puts it well: Object languages *allow* advantages but don't *provide* them. To use these advantages, you have to make the infamous paradigm shift. (Just make sure you are sitting down at the time!)

The techniques in the UML were to some degree designed to help people do good OO, but different techniques have different advantages.

- One of the most valuable techniques for learning OO is CRC cards (see page 75), which are not part of the UML, although they can and should be used with it. They were designed primarily for teaching people to work with objects. As such, CRC cards are deliberately different from traditional design techniques. Their emphasis on responsibilities and their lack of complex notation make CRC cards particularly valuable.

- Interaction diagrams (see Chapter 5) are very useful because they make the message structure very explicit and thus are useful for highlighting over-centralized designs, in which one object is doing all the work.

- Class diagrams (see Chapters 4 and 6), used to illustrate class models, are both good and bad for learning objects. Class models are comfortably similar to data models; many of the principles that make for a good data model also make for a good class model. The major problem in using class diagrams is that it is easy to develop a class model that is data oriented rather than being responsibility oriented.

- The concept of patterns (see page 33) has become vital to learning OO because using patterns gets you to concentrate on good OO designs and to learn by following an example. Once you have gotten the hang of some basic modeling techniques, such as simple class diagrams and interaction diagrams, it is time to start looking at patterns.

- Another important technique is iterative development (see Chapter 2). This technique does not help you learn OO in any direct way, but it is the key to exploiting OO effectively. If you do iterative development from the start, you will learn, in context, the right kind of process and begin to see why designers suggest doing things the way they do.

When you start using a technique, you tend to do it by the book. My recommendation is to begin with the simple notations that I talk about here, particularly with class diagrams. As you get comfortable, you can pick up the more advanced ideas as you need them. You may also find that you wish to extend the method.

Communicating with Domain Experts

One of our biggest challenges in development is that of building the *right* system—one that meets users' needs at a reasonable cost. This is made more difficult because we, with our jargon, have to communicate with users, who have their own, more arcane, jargon. (I did a lot of work in health care, and there the jargon isn't even in English!) Achieving good communication, along with good understanding of the users' world, is the key to developing good software.

The obvious technique to use in addressing this is use cases (see Chapter 3). A **use case** is a snapshot of one aspect of your system. The sum of all use cases is the external picture of your system, which goes a long way toward explaining what the system will do.

A good collection of use cases is central to understanding what your users want. Use cases also present a good vehicle for project planning, because they control iterative development, which is itself a valuable technique, since it gives regular feedback to the users about where the software is going.

Although use cases help with communication about surface things, it is also crucial to look at the deeper things. This involves learning how your domain experts understand their world.

Class diagrams (see Chapters 4 and 6) can be extremely valuable here, as long as you draw them from the *conceptual* perspective. In other words, you should treat each class as a concept in a user's mind. The class diagrams you draw are then not diagrams of data or of classes, but rather of the language of your users.

I have found activity diagrams (see Chapter 9) to be very useful in cases in which workflow processes are an important part of the users' world. Since they support parallel processes, activity diagrams can help you get away from unnecessary sequences. The way these diagrams deemphasize the links to classes, which can be a problem in later design, becomes an advantage during this more conceptual stage of the development process.

Looking for More Information

This book is not a complete and definitive reference to the UML, let alone OO analysis and design. There are a lot of words out there and a lot of worthwhile things to read. As I discuss the individual topics, I will talk about other books you should go to for more in-depth information on the ideas in the UML and on OOA&D in general.

Of course, your first step beyond this book should be the three amigos' books on the UML.

- Grady Booch led the work on the user's guide (Booch, Rumbaugh, and Jacobson 1999). This tutorial book explores ways in which you can use the UML to carry out various design tasks.
- Jim Rumbaugh led the effort on the reference manual (Rumbaugh, Jacobson, and Booch 1999). I often find this detailed reference to the UML very useful.
- Ivar Jacobson led work on the book that describes a process that works with the UML (Jacobson, Booch, and Rumbaugh 1999). I'll talk more about process issues in Chapter 2.

Of course, the three amigos' books are not the only ones you should read to learn about good OOA&D. My list of recommended books changes frequently; take a look at my home page for details.

If you are new to objects, I recommend my current favorite introductory book, Larman (1998). The author has a strong responsibility-driven approach to design that is worth following. If you want to know more about objects from a conceptual point of view, Martin and Odell (1998) is now available in a UML edition. Real-time developers should get a copy of Douglass (1998).

I also suggest that you read books on patterns for material that will take you beyond the basics. Now that the methods war is over, I think that patterns will be where most of the interesting material about analysis and design will appear. Inevitably, however, people will come up with new analysis and design techniques, and it is likely that they will talk about how these techniques can be used with the UML. This is another benefit of the UML; it encourages people to add new techniques without duplicating work that everyone else has done.

Chapter 2

An Outline Development Process

The UML is a modeling language, not a method. The UML has no notion of process, which is an important part of a method.

The title of this book is *UML Distilled*, so I could have safely ignored process. However, I don't believe that modeling techniques make any sense without knowing how they fit into a process. This is why I decided to discuss the process first, so you can see how an object-oriented development works. I call it an outline process because rather than trying to go into great detail, I'm offering just enough to give you a sense of the typical way in which a project that uses these techniques is run.

The three amigos have developed a merged process called the *Rational Unified Process*. (It used to be called Objectory.) This process is described in the amigos' process book (Jacobson, Booch, and Rumbaugh 1999).

As I discuss the outline process, I will use the terminology and outline framework of the Rational Unified Process. (I have to use something, and that seems as good as anything.) However, I have not tried to describe the Rational Unified Process; that is beyond the scope of this book. Rather, I'm describing a lightweight, low-ceremony process that is consistent with Rational's process. For full details on the Rational Unified Process, you should go to the amigos' process book or see Kruchten's overview (1999).

Although the Rational Unified Process contains details about what kinds of models to develop at the various stages in the process, I won't go into such details. Nor will I specify tasks, deliverables, and roles. My terminology is looser than that of the Rational Unified Process—that is the price one pays for lightweight description.

Whatever process discussion there is, don't forget that you can use *any* process with the UML. The UML is independent of process. You should pick something that is appropriate for your kind of project. Whatever process you use, you can use the UML to record the resulting analysis and design decisions.

Indeed, I don't believe that you can have a single process for software development. Various factors associated with software development lead you to various kinds of processes. These factors include the kind of software you are developing (real time, information system, desktop product), the scale (single developer, small team, 100-plus-member team), and so forth.

I believe that teams should grow their own processes, using published processes as advice rather than as standards to follow.

Overview of the Process

Figure 2-1 shows the high-level view of the development process.

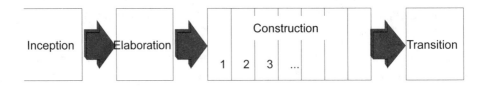

Figure 2-1: *Outline Development Process*

This process is an iterative and incremental development process, in that the software is not released in one big bang at the end of the project but is, instead, developed and released in pieces. The **construction** phase consists of many **iterations**, in which each iteration builds production-quality software, tested and integrated, that satisfies a subset of the requirements of the project.The delivery may be external, to early users, or purely internal. Each iteration contains all the usual lifecycle phases of analysis, design, implementation, and testing.

In principle, you can start at the beginning: Pick some functionality and build it, pick some other functionality, and so forth. However, it is worthwhile to spend some time planning.

The first two phases are inception and elaboration. During **inception**, you establish the business rationale for the project and decide on the scope of the project. This is where you get the commitment from the project sponsor to go further. In **elaboration**, you collect more detailed requirements, do high-level analysis and design to establish a baseline architecture, and create the plan for construction.

Even with this kind of iterative process, some work has to be left to the end, in the **transition** phase. This work can include beta testing, performance tuning, and user training.

Projects vary in how much **ceremony** they have. High-ceremony projects have a lot of formal paper deliverables, formal meetings, formal sign-offs. Low-ceremony projects might have an inception phase that consists of an hour's chat with the project's sponsor and a plan that sits on a spreadsheet. Naturally, the bigger the project, the more ceremony you need. The fundamentals of the phases still occur, but in very different ways.

I try to keep the ceremony to a minimum, and my discussion reflects that. There are plenty of high-ceremony processes to choose from elsewhere.

I've shown iterations in the construction phase, but not in the other phases. In fact, you can have iterations in all phases, and it is often a good idea to do so in a large phase. Construction is the key phase in which to iterate, however.

That's the high-level view. Now we will delve into the details so that we have enough information to see where the techniques discussed later in the book fit into the larger scheme of things. In doing this, I will talk a bit about these techniques and when to use them. You may find it a little confusing if you are unfamiliar with the techniques. If that's the case, skip those bits and come back to them later.

Inception

Inception can take many forms. For some projects, it's a chat at the coffee machine: "Have a look at putting our catalog of services on the Web." For bigger projects, it might be a full-fledged feasibility study that takes months.

During the inception phase, you work out the business case for the project—roughly how much it will cost and how much it will bring in. You will also need to get a sense of the project's scope. You may need to do some initial analysis to get a sense of the size of the project.

I don't tend to make a big deal of inception. Inception should be a few days' work to consider whether it is worth doing a few months' worth of deeper investigation during elaboration (see the next section). At this point, the project's sponsor agrees to no more than a serious look at the project.

Elaboration

So you have the go-ahead to start a project. At this stage, typically, you have only a vague idea of the requirements. For instance, you might be able to say:

> *We are going to build the next-generation customer support system for the Watts Galore Utility Company. We intend to use object-oriented technology to build a more flexible system that is more customer-oriented—specifically, one that will support consolidated customer bills.*

Of course, your requirements document will likely be more expansive than that, but it may not actually say very much more.

At this point, you want to get a better understanding of the problem.

- What is it you are actually going to build?
- How are you going to build it?

In deciding what issues to look into during this phase, you need to be driven, first and foremost, by the risks in your project. What things could derail you? The bigger the risk, the more attention you have to pay to it.

In my experience, risks can usefully be classified into four categories:

1. *Requirements risks.* What are the requirements of the system? The big danger is that you will build the wrong system, one that does not do what the customer needs.

2. *Technological risks.* What are the technological risks you have to face? Are you selecting technology that will actually do the job for you? Will the various pieces fit together?

3. *Skills risks.* Can you get the staff and expertise you need?

4. *Political risks.* Are there political forces that can get in the way and seriously affect your project?

There may be more in your case, but risks that fall into these four categories are nearly always present.

Dealing with Requirements Risks

Requirements are important and are where UML techniques can most obviously be brought to bear. The starting point is use cases. Use cases drive the whole development process.

I'll talk in detail about use cases in Chapter 3; here I'll just give you a brief description of what use cases are.

A use case is a typical interaction that a user has with the system in order to achieve a goal. Imagine the word processor that I am currently using. One use case would be "do a spell check"; another would be "create an index for a document."

The key element for a use case is that each one indicates a function that the user can understand and that has value for that user. A developer can respond with specifics. For instance:

> *It will take me two months to do the index function for you. I also have a use case to support grammar checking; I reckon that's three months. We have only three months to the release—which one would you like?*

Use cases provide the basis of communication between customers and developers in planning the project.

One of the most important things to do in the elaboration phase is to discover all the potential use cases for the system you are building. In practice, of course, you aren't going to get all of them. You want to get most, however, particularly the most important and riskiest ones. It's for this reason that, during the elaboration phase, you should schedule interviews with users for the purpose of gathering use cases.

Use cases do not need to be detailed. I usually find that a paragraph or three of descriptive text is sufficient. This text should be specific enough for the users to understand the basic idea and for the developers to have a broad sense of what lurks inside.

Use cases are not the whole picture, however. Another important task is to come up with the skeleton of a conceptual model of the domain. Within the heads of one or more users lies a picture of how the business operates. For instance:

> *Our customers may have several sites, and we provide several services to these sites. At the moment, a customer gets a bill for all services at a given site. We want that customer to be billed for all services at all sites. We call this consolidated billing.*

This passage contains the words "customer," "site," and "service." What do these terms mean? How do they fit together? A conceptual domain model starts to answer these questions and, at the same time, lays the foundation for the object model that will be used to represent the objects in the system later in the process. I use the term **domain model** to describe any model whose primary subject is the world that the computer system is supporting, whatever stage of the development process you are in.

Note that the Rational Unified Process defines the term "domain model" more narrowly; see Jacobson, Booch, and Rumbaugh (1999) for details. My usage follows that of most people I know in the object community.

I find two UML techniques particularly valuable in building conceptual domain models.

The main technique I use for domain models is the class diagram, drawn from a conceptual perspective (see Chapter 4). You can use these diagrams to lay out the concepts that the business experts use as they think about the business and to lay out the ways those experts link concepts together. In many ways, class diagrams are about defining a rigorous vocabulary to talk about the domain.

If the domain also has a strong workflow element, I like to describe this with activity diagrams (see Chapter 9). The key aspect of activity diagrams is that they encourage finding parallel processes, which is important in eliminating unnecessary sequences in business processes.

Some people like to use interaction diagrams (see Chapter 5) to explore how various roles interact in the business. By thinking about workers and activities together, they find it easier to gain an understanding of the process. I prefer to use activity diagrams to figure out what needs to be done first and to address who does what later.

Domain modeling can be a great adjunct to use cases. When I gather use cases, I like to bring in a domain expert and explore how that person thinks about the business, with the help of conceptual class diagrams and activity diagrams.

In this situation, I use minimal notation, I don't worry about rigor, and I make lots of informational notes on the diagram. I don't try to capture every detail. Instead, I focus on important issues and areas that imply risk. I draw lots of unconnected diagrams without worrying about consistency and interrelationships among diagrams.

I find that this process can quickly yield a lot of understanding. Armed with this understanding, I find that I can more easily identify the use cases for the various users.

After I've covered most of the relevant areas, I like to consolidate the various diagrams into a single consistent domain model. For this, I use one or two domain experts who like to get deeper into the modeling. I maintain a conceptual perspective but, at the same time, become more rigorous.

This model can then act as a starting point for building classes in the construction phase. If this model is large, I use packages to divide the model into chunks. I'll do consolidation for class and activity diagrams and perhaps draw a couple of state diagrams for classes that have interesting lifecycles.

You should think of this initial domain model as a skeleton, not as a high-level model. The term "high-level model" implies that a lot of details are missing. I have seen this mistake made in several situations, expressed as, for instance, "Don't show attributes on these models." The results are models with no substance. It's easy to see why developers deride such efforts.

You can't take the opposite approach and build a detailed model, however. If you do, it will take ages and you will die from analysis paralysis. The trick is to find and concentrate on the important details. Most of the details will be dealt with during iterative development. This is why I prefer to think of this model as a skeleton. The skeleton is the foundation of the rest of the model. It is detailed, but it is only a small part of the story.

Naturally, this does not tell you how to differentiate bone from flesh; that is the art of the skilled analyst, and I haven't figured out how to bottle that yet!

Domain modeling is also driven by the use cases as they become known. As use cases appear, the modeling team should look at them to assess whether they contain anything that could have a strong impact on the domain model. If so, they should explore further; if not, the use cases should be put aside for the time being.

The team that builds the domain model should be a small group (two to four people) that includes developers and domain experts. The smallest viable team would be one developer and one domain expert.

The team should work intensively during the elaboration period until it reaches closure on the model. During this period, the leadership should ensure that the team neither gets bogged down in details nor operates at so high a level that their feet don't touch the ground. Once they get the hang of what they are doing, bogging down is the biggest danger. A hard deadline works well in concentrating minds.

As part of understanding the requirements, you should build a prototype of any tricky parts of the use cases. Prototyping is a valuable technique for getting a better understanding of how more dynamic situations work.

I use prototyping whenever I'm uncomfortable about how a risky part of the system is really going to work. I prototype just enough so that I can understand enough to assess the risk and estimate how much effort it will take to do things. Usually, I don't prototype the whole picture; instead, I use the overall domain model to highlight areas that need prototyping.

I find that people new to the UML need to prototype more. This helps them gain familiarity in how the UML diagrams correspond to actual programming.

When you use a prototype, don't be constrained by the environment in which you will actually deliver. For instance, I have often gained a lot from analysis prototyping in Smalltalk, even if I am building a C++ system.

One of the most important elements in dealing with requirements risk is getting access to domain expertise. Lack of access to people who really know the domain is one of the commonest ways for projects to fail. It is worth investing considerable time and money to bring people who really know the domain into your team—the quality of the software will be directly proportional to their expertise. They need not be full time, but they need to be open-minded, have deep hands-on understanding, and be readily available for questions.

Dealing with Technological Risks

The most important thing to do in addressing technological risks is to build prototypes that try out the pieces of technology you are thinking of using.

For example, say you are using C++ and a relational database. You should build a simple application using C++ and the database together. Try out several tools and see which ones work best. Spend some time getting comfortable with the tools you are going to use.

Don't forget that the biggest technological risks are inherent in how the components of a design fit together rather than being present in any of the components themselves. You may know C++ well, and you may know relational databases well, but putting them together can be surprisingly hard. This is why it is very important to get all the components you intend to use and fit them together at this early stage of the process.

You should also address any architectural design decisions during this stage. These usually take the form of ideas of what the major components are and how they will be built. This is particularly important if you are contemplating a distributed system.

As part of this exercise, focus on any areas that look as though they will be difficult to change later. Try to do your design in a way that will allow you to change elements of the design relatively easily. Ask yourself these questions.

- What will happen if a piece of technology doesn't work?
- What if we can't connect two pieces of the puzzle?
- What is the likelihood of something going wrong? How would we cope if that happens?

As with the domain model, you should look at the use cases as they appear in order to assess whether they contain anything that could cripple your design. If you fear they may contain a "purple worm," investigate further.

During this process, you will typically use a number of UML techniques to sketch out your ideas and document the things you try. Don't try to be comprehensive at this point; brief sketches are all you need and, therefore, all you should use.

- Class diagrams (see Chapters 4 and 6) and interaction diagrams (see Chapter 5) are useful in showing how components communicate.
- Package diagrams (see Chapter 7) can show a high-level picture of the components at this stage.
- Deployment diagrams (see Chapter 10) can provide an overview of how pieces are distributed.

Dealing with Skills Risks

I often go to conferences and listen to case study talks given by people who have just done an object-oriented project. They usually answer the question: "What were your biggest mistakes?" with responses that always include "We should have got more training."

It never ceases to amaze me how companies embark on important OO projects with little experience and little thought to how to gain more. People worry about the costs of training, but they pay every penny as the project takes longer.

Training is a way to avoid making mistakes, because instructors have already made those mistakes. Making mistakes takes time, and time costs money. So you pay the same either way, but not having the training causes the project to take longer.

I'm not a big fan of formal training courses. I've taught many of them and designed some as well. I remain unconvinced that they are effective in teaching object-oriented skills. They give people an overview of what they need to know, but they don't really pass on the core skills that you need to do a serious project. A short training course can be useful, but it's only a beginning.

If you do go for a short training course, pay a lot of attention to the instructor. It is worth paying a lot extra for someone who is knowledgeable and entertaining, because you will learn a lot more in the process. Also, get your training in small chunks, just at the time you need it. If you don't apply what you have learned in a training course straight away, you will forget it.

The best way to acquire OO skills is through **mentoring**, in which you have an experienced developer work with your project for an extended period of time. The mentor shows you how to do things, watches what you do, and passes on tips and short bits of training.

A mentor will work with the specifics of your project and knows which bits of expertise to apply at the right time. In the early stages, a mentor is one of the team, helping you come up with a solution. As time goes on, you become more capable, and the mentor does more reviewing than doing. My goal as a mentor is to render myself unnecessary.

You can find mentors for specific areas or for the overall project. Mentors can be full time or part time. Many mentors like to work a week out of each month on each project; others find that too little. Look for a mentor with knowledge and the ability to transfer that knowledge. Your mentor may be the most important factor in your project's success; it is worth paying for quality.

If you can't get a mentor, consider a project review every couple of months or so. Under this setup, an experienced mentor comes in for a few days to review various aspects of the design. During this time, the reviewer can highlight any areas of concern, suggest additional ideas, and outline any useful techniques that the team may be unaware of. Although this does not give you the full benefits of a good mentor, it can be valuable in spotting key things that you can do better.

You can also supplement your skills by reading. Try to read a solid technical book at least once every other month. Even better, read it as part of a book group. Find a couple of other people who want to read the same book. Agree to read a few chapters a week, and spend an hour or two discussing those chapters with the others. By doing this, you can gain a better understanding of the book than by reading it on your own. If you are a manager, encourage this. Get a room for the group; give your staff the money to buy technical books; allocate time for a book group.

The patterns community has found book groups to be particularly valuable. Several patterns reading groups have appeared. Look at the patterns home page (<**http://www.hillside.net/patterns**>) for more information about these groups.

As you work through elaboration, keep an eye out for any areas in which you have no skills or experience. Plan to acquire the experience at the point at which you need it.

Dealing with Political Risks

I can't offer you any serious advice on this, because I'm not a skilled corporate politician. I strongly suggest that you find someone who is.

When Is Elaboration Finished?

My rule of thumb is that elaboration takes about a fifth of the total length of the project. Two events are key indicators that elaboration is complete.

- The developers can feel comfortable providing estimates, to the nearest person-week of effort, of how long it will take to build each use case.
- All the significant risks have been identified, and the major ones are understood to the extent that you know how you intend to deal with them.

Planning the Construction Phase

There are many ways to plan an iterative project. It's important that you develop a plan in order to be aware of progress and to signal progress through the team. The approach to planning I use is based on the techniques in *Extreme Programming Explained* (Beck 2000).

The essence of building a plan involves setting up a series of iterations for construction and defining the functionality to deliver in each iteration. Some people like to use small use cases and complete a use case within an iteration; others like to use larger use cases, doing some scenarios in one iteration and others later. The basic process is the same. I'll describe it with the smaller use cases.

During planning, I like to consider two groups of people: customers and developers.

Customers are the people who are going to use the system for an in-house development. For a shrink-wrap system, marketing people usually represent the customer. The key thing is that the customers are the people who can assess the business value of a use case being implemented.

The developers are the people who are going to build the system. They must understand the costs and effort involved in building a use case. So, they must be familiar with the development environment. Management usually cannot play this role, because you need recent technical experience to do this.

The first step is to categorize the use cases. I do this two ways.

First, the customer divides the use cases, according to their business value, into three piles: high, medium, and low. (Note that it's considered bad form to put everything in the "high" pile.) Then the customer records the contents of each category.

The developers then divide the use cases according to the development risk. For instance, "high risk" would be used for something that is very difficult to do, could have a big impact on the design of the system, or is just not well understood.

After this is done, the developers should estimate the length of time each use case will require, to the nearest person-week. In performing this estimate, assume that you need to do analysis, design, coding, unit testing, integration, and documentation. Assume also that you have a fully committed developer with no distractions (we'll add a fudge factor later).

Once your estimates are in place, you can assess whether you are ready to make the plan. Look at the use cases with high risk. If a lot of the project's time is tied up in these use cases, you need to do more elaboration.

The next step is to determine your iteration length. You want a fixed iteration length for the whole project so that you get a regular rhythm to the iteration delivery. An iteration should be long enough for you to do a handful of use cases. For Smalltalk, it can be as low as two to three weeks, for instance; for C++, it can be as high as six to eight weeks.

Now you can consider how much effort you have for each iteration.

Note that you will have made these estimates assuming a developer with no distractions. Obviously, this is never the case, so I allow for that with a load factor that is the difference between ideal time and the reality. You should measure this load factor by comparing estimates to actuals.

Now you can work out how fast you can go, which I term the project velocity. This is how much development you can do in an iteration. You calculate this by taking your number of developers, multiplying it by the iteration length, and then dividing the result by the load factor. For instance, given 8 developers, a 3-week iteration length, and a load factor of 2, you would have 12 ideal developer-weeks (8 * 3 * 1/2) of effort per iteration.

Add up your time for all use cases, divide by the effort per iteration, and add 1 for luck. The result is your first estimate of how many iterations you will need for your project.

The next step is to assign the use cases to iterations.

Use cases that carry high priority and/or development risk should be dealt with early. Do *not* put off risk until the end! You may need to split big use cases, and you will probably revise use case estimates in light of the order in which you are doing things. You can have less work to do than the effort in the iteration, but you should never schedule more than your effort allows.

For transition, allocate from 10 percent to 35 percent of the construction time for tuning and packaging for the delivery. (Use a higher figure if you are inexperienced with tuning and packaging in your current environment.)

Then add a contingency factor: 10 percent to 20 percent of the construction time, depending on how risky things look. Add this factor to the end of the transition phase. You should plan to deliver without using contingency time— that is, on your internal target date—but commit to deliver at the end of contingent time.

After following all of these guidelines, you should have a **release plan** that shows the use cases that will be done during each iteration. This plan symbolizes commitment among developers and users. This plan is not cast in stone— indeed, everyone should expect the plan to change as the project proceeds. Since it is a commitment between developers and users, however, changes must be made jointly.

As you can see from this discussion, use cases serve as the foundation for planning the project, which is why the UML puts a lot of emphasis on them.

Construction

Construction builds the system in a series of iterations. Each iteration is a mini-project. You do analysis, design, coding, testing, and integration for the use cases assigned to each iteration. You finish the iteration with a demo to the user and perform system tests to confirm that the use cases have been built correctly.

The purpose of this process is to reduce risk. Risk often appears because difficult issues are left to the end of the project. I have seen projects in which testing and integration are left to the end. Testing and integration are big tasks, and they always take longer than people think. Left to the end, they are hard and demoralizing. That's why I always encourage my clients to develop self-testing software (see sidebar).

The iterations within construction are both incremental and iterative.

- The iterations are *incremental* in function. Each iteration builds on the use cases developed in the previous iterations.
- The iterations are *iterative* in terms of the code base. Each iteration will involve rewriting some existing code to make it more flexible.

Refactoring (see sidebar) is a highly useful technique in iterating the code. It's a good idea to keep an eye on the amount of code thrown away in each iteration. Be suspicious if less than 10 percent of the previous code is discarded each time.

Integration should be a continuous process. For starters, full integration is part of the end of each iteration. However, integration can and should occur more frequently than that. A good practice is to do a full build and integration every day. By doing that every day, things never get so far out of sync that it becomes a problem to integrate them later.

A developer should integrate after every significant piece of work. Also, the full suite of unit tests should be run at each integration, to ensure full regression testing.

Self-Testing Software

The older I get, the more aggressive I get about testing. Testing should be a continuous process. No code should be written until you know how to test it. Once you have written it, write the tests for it. Until the tests work, you cannot claim to have finished writing the code.

Test code, once written, should be kept forever. Set up your test code so that you can run every test with a simple command line or GUI button push. The code should respond with either "OK" or a list of failures. Also, all tests should check their own results. There is nothing more time-wasting than having a test output a number, the meaning of which you have to research.

I do both unit and functional testing. Unit tests should be written by the developers, then organized on a package basis and coded to test the interfaces of all classes. I find that writing unit tests actually increases my programming speed.

Functional tests or system tests should be developed by a separate small team whose only job is testing. This team should take a black-box view of the system and take particular delight in finding bugs. (Sinister mustaches and cackling laughs are optional but desirable.)

There is a simple but powerful open source framework for unit testing: the xUnit family. For details, see the link from my home page.

When the Plan Goes Awry

The only thing you know for certain about a plan is that things aren't going to go according to it. Managing the plan is all about coping with those changes effectively.

A key feature of iterative development is that it is time-boxed—you are not allowed to slip any dates. Instead, use cases can be moved to a later iteration via negotiation and agreement with the customer. The point of this is to maintain a regular habit of hitting dates and to avoid the bad habit of slipping dates.

Refactoring

Have you come across the principle of software entropy? It suggests that programs start off in a well-designed state, but as new bits of functionality are tacked on, programs gradually lose their structure, eventually deforming into a mass of spaghetti.

Part of this is due to scale. You write a small program that does a specific job well. People ask you to enhance the program, and it gets more complex. Even if you try to keep track of the design, this can still happen.

One of the reasons that software entropy occurs is that when you add a new function to a program, you build on top of the existing program, often in a way that the existing program was not intended to support. In such a situation, you can either redesign the existing program to better support your changes, or you can work around those changes in your additions.

Although in theory it is better to redesign your program, this usually results in extra work because any rewriting of your existing program will introduce new bugs and problems. Remember the old engineering adage: "If it ain't broke, don't fix it!" However, if you don't redesign your program, the additions will be more complex than they should be.

Gradually, this extra complexity will exact a stiff penalty. Therefore, there is a trade-off: Redesigning causes short-term pain for longer-term gain. Schedule pressure being what it is, most people prefer to put their pain off to the future.

Refactoring is a term used to describe techniques that reduce the short-term pain of redesigning. When you refactor, you do not change the functionality of your program; rather, you change its internal structure in order to make it easier to understand and work with.

Refactoring changes are usually small steps: renaming a method, moving a field from one class to another, consolidating two similar methods into a superclass. Each step is tiny, yet a couple of hours' worth of performing these small steps can do a world of good to a program.

Refactoring is made easier by the following principles.

- Do not refactor a program and add functionality to it at the same time. Impose a clear separation between the two when you work. You might swap between them in short steps—for instance, half an hour refactoring, an hour adding a new function, and half an hour refactoring the code you just added.

- Make sure you have good tests in place before you begin refactoring.

- Take short, deliberate steps. Move a field from one class to another. Fuse two similar methods into a superclass. Test after each step. This may sound slow, but it avoids debugging and thus speeds you up.

You should refactor when you are adding a new function or fixing a bug. Don't set aside specific time for refactoring; instead, do a little every day.

For more information on refactoring, see Fowler (1999).

If you find yourself deferring too many use cases, it's time to redo the plan, including reestimating use case effort levels. By this stage, the developers should have a better idea of how long things will take. You should *expect* to alter the plan every two or three iterations.

Using the UML in Construction

All UML techniques are useful during this stage. Since I am going to refer to techniques I haven't had a chance to talk about yet, feel free to skip this section and come back to it later.

As you look to add a given use case, you first use it to determine what your scope is. A conceptual class diagram (see Chapter 4) can be useful to rough out some concepts for the use case and see how these concepts fit with the software that has already been built.

The advantage of these techniques at this stage is that they can be used in conjunction with the domain expert. As Brad Kain says: Analysis occurs only when the domain expert is in the room (otherwise it is pseudo-analysis).

To make the move to design, walk through how the classes will collaborate to implement the functionality required by each use case. I find that CRC cards and interaction diagrams are useful in exploring these interactions. These will expose responsibilities and operations that you can record on the class diagram.

Treat these designs as an initial sketch and as a tool with which to discuss design approaches with your colleagues. Once you are comfortable, it is time to move to code.

Inevitably, the unforgiving code will expose weaknesses in the design. Don't be afraid to change the design in response to this learning. If the change is serious, use the notations to discuss ideas with your colleagues.

Once you have built the software, you can use the UML to help document what you have done. For this, I find UML diagrams useful for getting an overall understanding of a system. In doing this, however, I should stress that I do not believe in producing detailed diagrams of the whole system. To quote Ward Cunningham (1996):

> *Carefully selected and well-written memos can easily substitute for traditional comprehensive design documentation. The latter rarely shines except in isolated spots. Elevate those spots... and forget about the rest.*

I believe that detailed documentation should be generated from the code (like, for instance, JavaDoc). You should write additional documentation to highlight important concepts. Think of these as comprising a first step for the reader before he or she goes into the code-based details. I like to structure these as prose documents, short enough to read over a cup of coffee, using UML diagrams to help illustrate the discussion.

I use a package diagram (see Chapter 7) as my logical road map of the system. This diagram helps me understand the logical pieces of the system and see the dependencies (and keep them under control). A deployment diagram (see Chapter 10), which shows the high-level physical picture, may also prove useful at this stage.

Within each package, I like to see a specification-perspective class diagram. I don't show every operation on every class. I show only the associations and key attributes and operations that help me understand what is in there. This class diagram acts as a graphical table of contents.

If a class has complex lifecycle behavior, I draw a state diagram (see Chapter 8) to describe it. I do this only if the behavior is sufficiently complex, which I find doesn't happen often. More common are complicated interactions among classes, for which I draw interaction diagrams.

I'll often include some important code, written in a literate program style. If a particularly complex algorithm is involved, I'll consider using an activity diagram (see Chapter 9), but only if it gives me more understanding than the code alone.

If I find concepts that are coming up repeatedly, I use patterns (see sidebar) to capture the basic ideas.

Transition

The point of iterative development is to do the whole development process regularly so that the development team gets used to delivering finished code. But some things should not be done early. A prime example is optimization.

Optimization reduces the clarity and extensibility of the system in order to improve performance. That is a trade-off you need to make—after all, a system does have to be fast enough to meet users' requirements. But optimizing too early makes development tougher, so this is one thing that does need to be left to the end.

During transition, there is no development to add functionality, unless it is small and absolutely essential. There *is* development to fix bugs. A good example of a transition phase is that time between the beta release and the final release of a product.

When to Use Iterative Development

You should use iterative development only on projects that you want to succeed.

Patterns

The UML tells you how to express an object-oriented design. **Patterns** look, instead, at the results of the process: example models.

Many people have commented that projects have problems because the people involved were not aware of designs that are well known to those with more experience. Patterns describe common ways of doing things. They are collected by people who spot repeating themes in designs. These people take each theme and describe it so that other people can read the pattern and see how to apply it.

Let's look at an example. Say you have some objects running in a process on your desktop, and they need to communicate with other objects running in another process. Perhaps this process is also on your desktop; perhaps it resides elsewhere. You don't want the objects in your system to have to worry about finding other objects on the network or executing remote procedure calls.

What you can do is create a *proxy* object within your local process for the remote object. The proxy has the same interface as the remote object. Your local objects talk to the proxy using the usual in-process message sends. The proxy then is responsible for passing any messages on to the real object, wherever it might reside.

Figure 2-2 is a class diagram (see Chapter 4) that illustrates the structure of the *Proxy* pattern.

Proxies are a common technique used in networks and elsewhere. People have a lot of experience using proxies in terms of knowing how they can be used, what advantages they can bring, their limitations, and how to implement them. Methods books like this one don't discuss this knowledge; all they discuss is how you can diagram a proxy. Although useful, it is not as useful as discussing the experience involving proxies.

In the early 1990s, some people began to capture this experience. They formed a community interested in writing patterns. These people sponsor conferences and have produced several books.

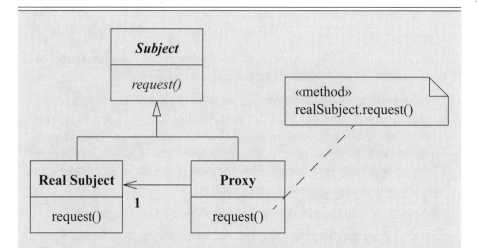

Figure 2-2: *Structure of Proxy Design Pattern*

The most famous patterns book to emerge from this group is the Gang of Four book (Gamma, Helm, Johnson, and Vlissides 1995), which discusses 23 design patterns in detail.

If you want to know about proxies, this is the source. The Gang of Four book spends 10 pages on the subject, giving details about how the objects work together, the benefits and limitations of the pattern, common variations and usages, and implementation tips for Smalltalk and C++.

Proxy is a design pattern because it describes a design technique. Patterns can also exist in other areas. Say you are designing a system for managing risk in financial markets. You need to understand how the value of a portfolio of stocks changes over time. You could do this by keeping a price for each stock and timestamping the price. However, you also want to be able to consider the risk in hypothetical situations (for instance, "What will happen if the price of oil collapses?").

To do this, you can create a *Scenario* that contains a whole set of prices for stocks. Then you can have separate *Scenarios* for the prices last week, your best guess for next week, your guess for next week if oil prices collapse, and so forth. This *Scenario* pattern (see Figure 2-3) is an analysis pattern because it describes a piece of domain modeling.

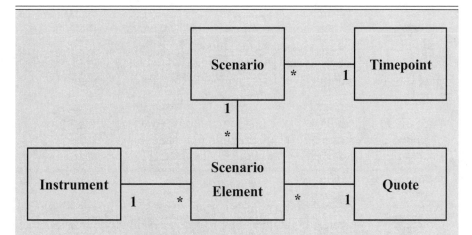

Figure 2-3: *Scenario Analysis Pattern*

Analysis patterns are valuable because they give you a better start when you work with a new domain. I started collecting analysis patterns because I was frustrated by new domains. I knew I wasn't the first person to model them, yet each time I had to start with a blank sheet of paper.

The interesting thing about analysis patterns is that they crop up in unusual places. When I started working on a project to do corporate financial analysis, I was enormously helped by a set of patterns I had previously discovered in health care.

See Fowler (1997) to learn more about *Scenario* and other analysis patterns.

A pattern is much more than a model. A pattern must also include the reason why it is the way it is. It is often said that a pattern is a solution to a problem. The pattern must make the problem clear, explain why it solves the problem, and also explain in what circumstances it works and does not work.

Patterns are important because they are the next stage beyond understanding the basics of a language or a modeling technique. Patterns give you a series of solutions and also show you what makes a good model and how you go about constructing a model. They teach by example.

When I started out, I wondered why I had to invent things from scratch. Why didn't I have handbooks to show me how to do common things? The patterns community is trying to build these handbooks.

When to Use Patterns

Whenever you try to develop something in analysis, design, coding, or project management, you should search for any available patterns that might help you.

Where to Find Out More

The books I mentioned earlier are a good starting point on patterns. To go further, take a look at the patterns home page: **<http://www.hillside.net/patterns>**. This gives you good up-to-date information on the state of the patterns world.

Perhaps that's a bit glib, but as I get older, I get more aggressive about using iterative development. Done well, it is an essential technique, which you can use to expose risk early and to obtain better control over development. It is not the same as having no management (although, to be fair, I should point out that some have used it that way). It does need to be well planned. But it is a solid approach, and every OO development book encourages using it—for good reason.

Where to Find Out More

There are lots of books on process. One of my two favorites is Cockburn (1998), because he does a good job on focusing on the key issues in a short book. As such, I recommend this as a first book on managing an OO project. The other is McConnell (1996), which provides an in-depth look at best practices.

To find out more about the Rational Unified Process: Kruchten (1999) is a concise overview, while Jacobson, Booch, and Rumbaugh (1999) is the best source for more details.

If you are interested in a lightweight yet disciplined approach, take a look at Kent Beck's "extreme programming." It is a very different approach that emphasizes strong testing and evolutionary design. See **<http://xprogramming.com>** and Kent's book (Beck 2000). This is one of a new breed of "agile" methodologies; see **<http://martinfowler.com/articles/newMethodology.html>** for an overview of these.

Chapter 3

Use Cases

Use cases are interesting phenomena. For a long time, in both object-oriented and traditional development, people used typical interactions to help them understand requirements. However, these scenarios were treated very informally—always done but rarely documented. Ivar Jacobson is well known for changing this with his Objectory method and associated book (his first one).

Jacobson raised the visibility of the use case to the extent that it became a primary element in project development and planning. Since his book was published (1992), the object community has adopted use cases to a remarkable degree. My practice has certainly improved since I started using use cases in this manner.

So what is a use case?

I won't answer this question head-on. Instead, I'll sneak up on it from behind by first describing a scenario.

A **scenario** is a sequence of steps describing an interaction between a user and a system. So if we have a Web-based on-line store, we might have a Buy a Product scenario that would say this:

> *The customer browses the catalog and adds desired items to the shopping basket. When the customer wishes to pay, the customer describes the shipping and credit card information and confirms the sale. The system checks the authorization on*

the credit card and confirms the sale both immediately and with a follow-up email.

This scenario is one thing that can happen. However, the credit card authorization might fail. This would be a separate scenario.

A **use case**, then, is a set of scenarios tied together by a common user goal. In the current situation, you would have a Buy a Product use case with the successful purchase and the authorization failure as two of the use case's scenarios. Other, alternative paths for the use case would be further scenarios. Often, you find that a use case has a common all-goes-well case, and many alternatives that may include things going wrong and also alternative ways that things go well.

Cockburn (2001) suggests a simple format for capturing a use case that describes its *main success scenario* as a sequence of numbered steps and the *extensions* as variations on that sequence, as shown in Figure 3-1.

Buy a Product

Main Success Scenario:
1. Customer browses through catalog and selects items to buy
2. Customer goes to check out
3. Customer fills in shipping information (address; next-day or 3-day delivery)
4. System presents full pricing information, including shipping
5. Customer fills in credit card information
6. System authorizes purchase
7. System confirms sale immediately
8. System sends confirming email to customer

Extensions:
3a: Customer is regular customer
    3a1: System displays current shipping, pricing, and billing information
    3a2: Customer may accept or override these defaults, returns to MSS at step 6
6a: System fails to authorize credit purchase
    6a1: Customer may re-enter credit card information or may cancel.

Figure 3-1: *Example Use Case Text*

There is a lot of variation as far as how you might describe the contents of a use case; the UML does not specify any standard. There are also additional sections you can add. For example, you can add a line for preconditions, which are things that should be true when the use case can start. Take a look at the various books that address use cases, and add the elements that make sense for you. Don't include everything, just those things that really seem to help.

An important example of this is how you divide up use cases. Consider another scenario for on-line purchase, one in which the purchaser is already known to the system as a regular customer. Some people would consider this to be a third scenario, whereas others would make this a separate use case. You can also use one of the use case relationships, which I'll describe later.

The amount of detail you need depends on the risk in the use case: The more risk, the more detail you need. Often I find that I go into details only for a few use cases during elaboration, and the rest contain no more than the use case in Figure 3-1. During iteration, you add more detail as you need it to implement the use case. You don't have to write all of the detail down; verbal communication is often very effective.

Use Case Diagrams

In addition to introducing use cases as primary elements in software development, Jacobson (1994) also introduced a diagram for visualizing use cases. The **use case diagram** is also now part of the UML.

Many people find this kind of diagram useful. However, I must stress that you don't need to draw a diagram to use use cases. One of the most effective projects I know that used use cases involved keeping each one on an index card and sorting the cards into piles to show what needed building in each iteration.

Figure 3-2 shows some of the use cases for a financial trading system.

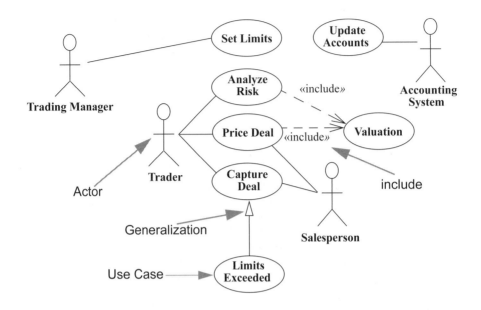

Figure 3-2: *Use Case Diagram*

Actors

An **actor** is a role that a user plays with respect to the system. There are four actors in Figure 3-2: Trading Manager, Trader, Salesperson, and Accounting System. (Yes, I know it would be better to use the word "role," but apparently, there was a mistranslation from the Swedish.)

There will probably be many traders in the given organization, but as far as the system is concerned, they all play the same role. A user may also play more than one role. For instance, one senior trader may play the Trading Manager role and also be a regular trader; a Trader may also be a Salesperson. When dealing with actors, it is important to think about roles rather than people or job titles.

Actors carry out use cases. A single actor may perform many use cases; conversely, a use case may have several actors performing it.

In practice, I find that actors are most useful when trying to come up with the use cases. Faced with a big system, it can often be difficult to come up with a list of use cases. It is easier in those situations to arrive at the list of actors first, and then try to work out the use cases for each actor.

Actors don't need to be human, even though actors are represented as stick figures within a use case diagram. An actor can also be an external system that needs some information from the current system. In Figure 3-2, we can see the need to update the accounts for the Accounting System.

There are several variations on what people show as actors. Some people show every external system or human actor on the use case diagram; others prefer to show the initiator of the use case. I prefer to show the actor that gets value from the use case, which some people refer to as the primary actor.

However, I don't take this too far. I'm happy to see the accounting system get value, without trying to figure out the human actor that gets value from the accounting system—that would entail modeling the accounting system itself. That said, you should always question use cases with system actors, find out what the real user goals are, and consider alternative ways of meeting those goals.

When I'm working with actors and use cases, I don't worry too much about what the exact relationships are among them. Most of the time, what I'm really after is the use cases; the actors are just a way to get there. As long as I get all the use cases, I'm not worried about the details of the actors.

There are some situations in which it can be worth tracking the actors later.

- The system may need configuring for various kinds of users. In this case, each kind of user is an actor, and the use cases show you what each actor needs to do.
- Tracking who wants use cases can help you negotiate priorities among various actors.

Some use cases don't have clear links to specific actors. Consider a utility company. Clearly, one of its use cases is Send Out Bill. It's not so easy to identify an associated actor, however. No particular user role requests a bill. The bill is sent to the customer, but the customer wouldn't object if it didn't happen. The best guess at an actor here is the Billing Department, in that it gets value from the use case. But Billing is not usually involved in playing out the use case.

Be aware that some use cases will not pop out as a result of the process of thinking about the use cases for each actor. If that happens, don't worry too much. The important thing is understanding the use cases and the user goals they satisfy.

A good source for identifying use cases is external events. Think about all the events from the outside world to which you want to react. A given event may cause a system reaction that does not involve users, or it may cause a reaction primarily from the users. Identifying the events that you need to react to will help you identify the use cases.

Use Case Relationships

In addition to the links among actors and use cases, you can show several kinds of relationships between use cases.

The **include** relationship occurs when you have a chunk of behavior that is similar across more than one use case and you don't want to keep copying the description of that behavior. For instance, both Analyze Risk and Price Deal require you to value the deal. Describing deal valuation involves a fair chunk of writing, and I hate copy-and-paste. So I spun off a separate Value Deal use case for this situation and referred to it from the original use cases.

You use **use case generalization** when you have one use case that is similar to another use case but does a bit more. In effect, this gives us another way of capturing alternative scenarios.

In our example, the basic use case is Capture Deal. This is the case in which all goes smoothly. Things can upset the smooth capture of a deal, however. One is when a limit is exceeded—for instance, the maximum amount the trading organization has established for a particular customer. Here we don't perform the usual behavior associated with the given use case; we carry out an alternative.

We could put this variation within the Capture Deal use case as an alternative, as with the Buy a Product use case I described earlier. However, we may feel that this alternative is sufficiently different to deserve a separate use case. We put the alternative path in a specialized use case that refers to the base use case. The specialized use case can override any part of the base use case, although it should still be about satisfying the same essential user goal.

A third relationship, which I haven't shown on Figure 3-2, is called **extend**. Essentially, this is similar to generalization but with more rules to it.

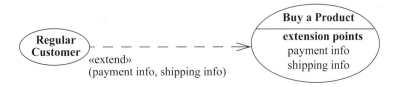

Figure 3-3: *Extend Relationship*

With this construct, the extending use case may add behavior to the base use case, but this time the base use case must declare certain "extension points," and the extending use case may add additional behavior only at those extension points. (See Figure 3-3.)

A use case may have many extension points, and an extending use case may extend one or more of these extension points. You indicate which ones on the line between the use cases on the diagram.

Both generalization and extend allow you to split up a use case. During elaboration, I often split any use case that's getting too complicated. I split during the construction stage of the project if I find that I can't build the whole use case in one iteration. When I split, I like to do the normal case first and the variations later.

Apply the following rules.

- Use *include* when you are repeating yourself in two or more separate use cases and you want to avoid repetition.

- Use *generalization* when you are describing a variation on normal behavior and you wish to describe it casually.

- Use *extend* when you are describing a variation on normal behavior and you wish to use the more controlled form, declaring your extension points in your base use case.

Business and System Use Cases

A common problem that can happen with use cases is that by focusing on the interaction between a user and the system, you can neglect situations in which a change to a business process may be the best way to deal with the problem.

Often you hear people talk about system use cases and business use cases. The terms are not precise, but the general usage is that a system use case is an interaction with the software, whereas a business use case discusses how a business responds to a customer or an event.

I don't like to get too bogged down in this issue. In the early stages of elaboration, I lean more toward business use cases, but I find system use cases more useful for planning. I find it useful to think about business use cases, particularly to consider other ways to meet an actor's goal.

In my work, I focus on business use cases first, and then I come up with system use cases to satisfy them. By the end of the elaboration period, I expect to have at least one set of system use cases for each business use case I have identified—at minimum, for the business use cases I intend to support in the first delivery.

When to Use Use Cases

I can't imagine a situation now in which I would not use use cases. They are an essential tool in requirements capture and in planning and controlling an iterative project. Capturing use cases is one of the primary tasks of the elaboration phase.

Most of your use cases will be generated during that phase of the project, but you will uncover more as you proceed. Keep an eye out for them at all times. Every use case is a potential requirement, and until you have captured a requirement, you cannot plan to deal with it.

Some people list and discuss the use cases first, then do some modeling. I've also found that conceptual modeling with users helps uncover use cases. So I tend to do use cases and conceptual modeling at the same time.

It is important to remember that use cases represent an *external* view of the system. As such, don't expect any correlations between use cases and the classes inside the system.

How many use cases should you have? During a recent OOPSLA panel discussion, several use case experts said that for a 10-person-year project, they would expect around a dozen use cases. These are base use cases; each use case would have many scenarios and many variant use cases. I've also seen projects of similar size with more than a hundred separate use cases. (If you count the variant use cases for a dozen use cases, the numbers end up about the same.) As ever, use what works for you.

The more I see of use cases, though, the less valuable the use case diagram seems to be. With use cases, concentrate your energy on the text of the use cases rather than the diagram. Despite the fact that the UML has nothing to say about the use case text, it really is the text that contains all of the value in the technique.

Where to Find Out More

For a long time, Alistair Cockburn has been one of the most listened-to voices on use cases. Finally he's put his use case thoughts into a book: Cockburn (2001). As one use case expert says: "[J]ust throw away everything else you've read about use cases and get his book." (Please make an exception for the book you're holding.) Cockburn maintains a web site at <**http://use-cases.org/**>.

Constantine and Lockwood (2000) provides a convincing process for deriving user interfaces from use cases; see also <**http://foruse.com/**>.

Chapter 4

Class Diagrams: The Essentials

The class diagram technique has become truly central within object-oriented methods. Virtually every method has included some variation on this technique.

The class diagram is not only widely used, but also subject to the greatest range of modeling concepts. Although the basic elements are needed by everyone, the advanced concepts are used less often. Therefore, I've broken my discussion of class diagrams into two parts: the essentials (this chapter) and the advanced (see Chapter 6).

A **class diagram** describes the types of objects in the system and the various kinds of static relationships that exist among them. There are two principal kinds of static relationships:

- **associations** (for example, a customer may rent a number of videos)
- **subtypes** (a nurse is a kind of person)

Class diagrams also show the attributes and operations of a class and the constraints that apply to the way objects are connected.

Figure 4-1 shows a typical class diagram.

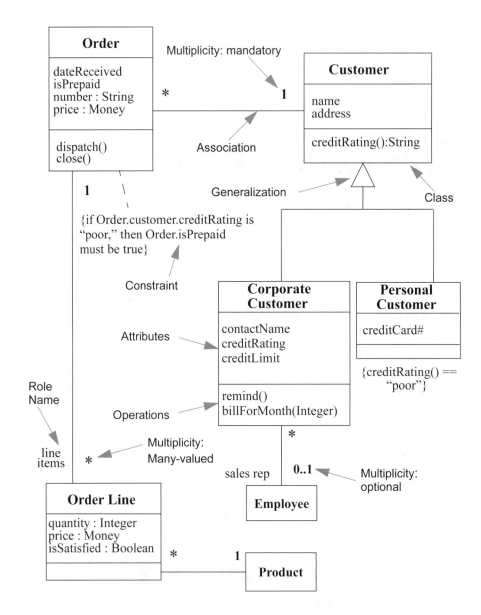

Figure 4-1: *Class Diagram*

Perspectives

Before I begin describing class diagrams, I would like to bring out an important subtlety in the way people use them. This subtlety is usually undocumented but has an impact on the way you should interpret a diagram, for it very much concerns what it is you are describing with a model.

Following the lead of Steve Cook and John Daniels (1994), I say that there are three perspectives you can use in drawing class diagrams—or indeed any model, but this breakdown is most noticeable in connection with class diagrams.

- **Conceptual**. If you take the conceptual perspective, you draw a diagram that represents the concepts in the domain under study. These concepts will naturally relate to the classes that implement them, but there is often no direct mapping. Indeed, a conceptual model should be drawn with little or no regard for the software that might implement it, so it can be considered language-independent. (Cook and Daniels call this the essential perspective.)

- **Specification**. Now we are looking at software, but we are looking at the interfaces of the software, not the implementation. Object-oriented development puts a great emphasis on the difference between interface and implementation, but this is often overlooked in practice because the notion of class in an OO language combines both interface and implementation. This is a shame, because the key to effective OO programming is to program to a class's interface rather than to its implementation. There is a good discussion of this in the first chapter of Gamma, Helm, Johnson, and Vlissides (1995). You often hear the word "type" used to talk about an interface of a class; a type can have many classes that implement it, and a class can implement many types.

- **Implementation**. In this view, we really do have classes and we are laying the implementation bare. This is probably the perspective used most often, but in many ways the specification perspective is often a better one to take.

Understanding perspective is crucial to both drawing and reading class diagrams. Unfortunately, the lines between the perspectives are not sharp, and most modelers do not take care to get their perspective sorted out when they are drawing. Although I've found that this often does not matter too much between the conceptual perspective and the specification perspective, it is very important to separate the specification perspective and the implementation perspective.

As I talk about class diagrams further, I will stress how each element of the technique depends heavily on the perspective.

Perspective is not part of the formal UML, but I have found it extremely valuable when modeling and when reviewing models. The UML can be used with all three perspectives. By tagging classes with a stereotype (see page 80), you can provide an indication of the perspective. You mark classes with «implementation class» to show the implementation perspective, and with «type» for the specification and conceptual perspectives.

Associations

Figure 4-1 shows a simple class model that would not surprise anyone who has worked with order processing. I'll describe each of the pieces and talk about how you would interpret them from the various perspectives.

I'll begin with the associations. **Associations** represent relationships between instances of classes (a person works for a company; a company has a number of offices).

From the **conceptual** perspective, associations represent conceptual relationships between classes. The diagram indicates that an Order has to come from a single Customer and that a Customer may make several Orders over time. Each of these Orders has several Order Lines, each of which refers to a single Product.

Each association has two **association ends**; each end is attached to one of the classes in the association. An end can be explicitly named with a label. This label is called a **role name**. (Association ends are often called **roles**.)

In Figure 4-1, the Order Line end of the association from Order is called *line items*. If there is no label, you name an end after the target class—so, for instance, the Customer end of the association from Order would be called *customer*.

An association end also has **multiplicity**, which is an indication of how many objects may participate in the given relationship. In Figure 4-1, the * on the Order end of the association with Customer indicates that a Customer may have many Orders associated with it, whereas the **1** on the other end indicates that an Order comes from only one Customer.

In general, the multiplicity indicates lower and upper bounds for the participating objects. The * represents the range *0..infinity*: A Customer need not have placed an Order, and there is no upper limit (in theory, at least!) to the number of Orders a Customer may place. The **1** stands for *1..1*: An Order must have been placed by exactly one Customer.

The most common multiplicities in practice are 1, *, and 0..1 (you can have either none or one). For a more general multiplicity, you can have a single number (such as *11* for players on a cricket team), a range (such as *2..4* for players of a canasta game), or discrete combinations of numbers and ranges (such as *2, 4* for doors in a car before the onset of minivans).

Within the **specification** perspective, associations represent responsibilities.

Figure 4-1 implies that there are one or more methods associated with Customer that will tell me what orders a given Customer has made. Similarly, there are methods within Order that will let me know which Customer placed a given Order and what Line Items are on an Order.

If there are standard conventions for naming these query methods, I can probably infer from the diagram what these methods are called. For example, I may have a convention that says that single-valued relationships are implemented with a method that returns the related object, and that multivalued relationships are implemented with an iterator into a collection of the related objects.

Working with a naming convention like this in Java, for instance, I can infer the following interface for an Order class:

```
class Order {
    public Customer getCustomer();
    public Set getOrderLines();

    ...
```

Obviously, programming conventions will vary from place to place and will not indicate every method, but they can be very useful in finding your way around.

An association also implies some responsibility for updating the relationship. There should be a way of relating the Order to the Customer. Again, the details are not shown; it could be that you specify the Customer in the constructor for the Order. Or, perhaps there is an *addOrder* method associated with Customer. You can make this more explicit by adding operations to the class box, as we will see later.

These responsibilities do *not* imply data structure, however. From a specification-level diagram, I can make no assumptions about the data structure of the classes. I cannot and should not be able to tell whether the Order class contains a pointer to Customer, or whether the Order class fulfills its responsibility by executing some selection code that asks each Customer whether it refers to a given Order. The diagram indicates only the interface—nothing more.

If this were an **implementation** model, we would now imply that there are pointers in both directions between the related classes. The diagram would now say that Order has a field that is a collection of pointers to Order Lines and also has a pointer to Customer. In Java, we could infer something like the following:

```
class Order {
    private Customer _customer;
    private Set _orderLines;
class Customer {
    private Set _orders;
```

In this case, most people assume that accessing operations are provided as well, but you can be sure only by looking at the operations on the class.

Now take a look at Figure 4-2. It is basically the same as Figure 4-1 except that I have added a couple of arrows on the association lines. These arrows indicate **navigability**.

In a specification model, this would indicate that an Order has a responsibility to tell you which Customer it is for, but a Customer has no corresponding ability to tell you which Orders it has. Instead of symmetrical responsibilities, we now have responsibilities on only one end of the line. In an implementation diagram, this would indicate that Order contains a pointer to Customer, but Customer would not have a pointer to Order.

As you can see, navigability is an important part of implementation and specification diagrams. I don't think that navigability serves any useful purpose on conceptual diagrams, however.

You will often see a conceptual diagram that first appears with no navigabilities. Then the navigabilities are added as part of the shift to the specification and implementation perspectives. Note also that the navigabilities are likely to be different between specification and implementation.

If a navigability exists in only one direction, we call the association a **unidirectional association**. A **bidirectional association** contains navigabilities in both directions. The UML says that you treat associations without arrows to mean that either the navigability is unknown or the association is bidirectional. Your project should settle on one or the other meaning. I prefer it to mean "undecided" for specification and implementation models.

Bidirectional associations include an extra constraint, which is that the two navigations are inverses of each other. This is similar to the notion of inverse functions in math. In the context of Figure 4-2, this means that every Line Item associated with an Order must be associated with the original Order. Similarly, if you take an Order Line and look at the Line Items for its associated Order, you should see the original Order Line in the collection. This property holds true within all three perspectives.

There are several ways of naming associations. Traditional data modelers like to name an association using a verb phrase so that the relationship can be used in a sentence. Most object modelers prefer to use nouns to name the role of one or the other of the ends, since that corresponds better to responsibilities and operations.

Some people name every association. I choose to name an association only when doing so improves understanding. I've seen too many associations with names like "has" or "is related to." If there is no name on the end, I consider the name of the end to be the name of the attached class, as I indicated previously.

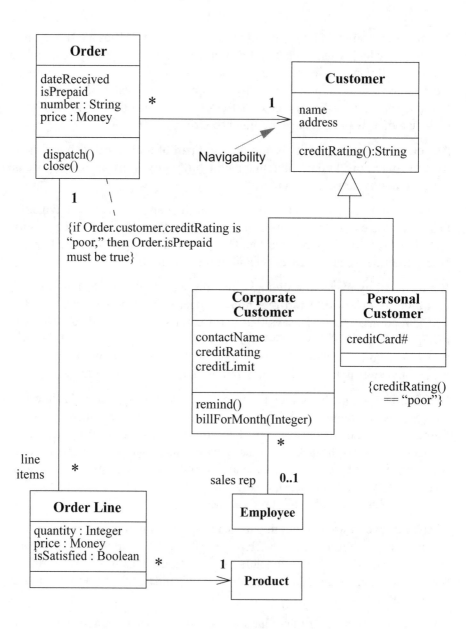

Figure 4-2: *Class Diagram with Navigabilities*

An association represents a permanent link between two objects. That is, the link exists during the whole lives of the objects, although the instances that are connected may change over time (or, in an optional association, be empty). So a parameter reference, or the creation of an object, does not imply an association; you model those with dependencies (see Chapters 6 and 7).

Attributes

Attributes are very similar to associations.

At the conceptual level, a Customer's name attribute indicates that Customers have names. At the specification level, this attribute indicates that a Customer object can tell you its name and has a way of setting a name. At the implementation level, a Customer has a **field** (also called an instance variable or a data member) for its name.

Depending on the detail in the diagram, the notation for an attribute can show the attribute's name, type, and default value. The UML syntax is *visibility name: type = defaultValue*, where *visibility* is the same as for operations, described in the next section.

So what is the difference between an attribute and an association?

From the conceptual perspective, there is no difference. An attribute carries just another kind of notation that you can use if it seems convenient. Attributes are usually single-valued. Usually, a diagram doesn't indicate whether an attribute is optional or mandatory, although you can do this by putting the multiplicity after the attribute name in square brackets—for example, *dateReceived[0..1] : Date*.

The difference occurs at the specification and implementation levels. Attributes imply navigability from the type to the attribute only. Furthermore, it is implied that the type contains solely its own copy of the attribute object, implying that any type used as an attribute has value rather than reference semantics.

I'll talk about value and reference types later on. For the moment, it's best to think of attributes as small, simple classes, such as strings, dates, money objects, and non-object values, such as *int* and *real*.

Operations

Operations are the processes that a class knows to carry out.

Operations most obviously correspond to the methods on a class. At the specification level, operations correspond to public methods on a type. Normally, you don't show those operations that simply manipulate attributes, because they can usually be inferred. You may need to indicate, however, whether a given attribute is read-only or frozen (that is, its value never changes). In the implementation model, you may want to show private and protected operations, as well.

The full UML syntax for operations is

visibility name (parameter-list) : return-type-expression {property-string}

where

- *visibility* is + (public), # (protected), or – (private)
- *name* is a string
- *parameter-list* contains comma-separated parameters whose syntax is similar to that for attributes: *direction name: type = default value.* The only extra element is *direction*, which is used to show whether the parameter is used for input (*in*), output (*out*), or both (*inout*). If there is no *direction* value, it's assumed to be *in*.
- *return-type-expression* is a comma-separated list of return types. Most people use only one return type, but multiple return types are allowed.
- *property-string* indicates property values that apply to the given operation

An example operation on account might be: + *balanceOn (date: Date) : Money.*

Within conceptual models, you shouldn't use operations to specify the interface of a class. Instead, use them to indicate the principal responsibilities of that class, perhaps using a couple of words summarizing a CRC responsibility (see Chapter 5).

I often find it useful to distinguish between operations that change the state of a class and those that don't. UML defines a **query** as an operation that gets a value from a class without changing the system state—in other words, without side effects. You can mark such an operation with the constraint {query}. I refer to operations that do change state as **modifiers**.

I find it helpful to highlight queries. Queries can be executed in any order, but the sequence of modifiers is more important. It's my practice to avoid returning values from modifiers, in order to keep them separate.

Other terms you sometimes see are getting methods and setting methods. A **getting method** returns a value from a field (and does nothing else). A **setting method** puts a value into a field (and does nothing else). From the outside, a client should not be able to tell whether a query is a getting method or if a modifier is a setting method. Knowledge of getting and setting methods is entirely internal to the class.

Another distinction is between operation and method. An **operation** is something that is invoked on an object (the procedure call), whereas a **method** is the body of procedure. The two are different when you have polymorphism. If you have a supertype with three subtypes, each of which overrides the supertype's "foo" operation, you have one operation and four methods that implement it.

People usually use operation and method interchangeably, but there are times when it is useful to be precise about the difference. Sometimes, people distinguish them by using the terms *method call* or *method declaration* (for operation) and *method body*.

Languages have their own naming conventions. In C++, operations are called *member functions*, whereas Smalltalk calls operations *methods*. C++ also uses the term *members of a class* to mean a class's operations and methods. UML uses the term *feature* to mean either an attribute or an operation.

Generalization

A typical example of **generalization** involves the personal and corporate customers of a business. They have differences but also many similarities. The similarities can be placed in a general Customer class (the supertype), with Personal Customer and Corporate Customer as subtypes.

This phenomenon is also subject to different interpretations at the different levels of modeling. Conceptually, we can say that Corporate Customer is a subtype of Customer if all instances of Corporate Customer are also, by definition, instances of Customer. A Corporate Customer is then a special kind of

Customer. The key idea is that everything we say about a Customer—associations, attributes, operations—is true also for a Corporate Customer.

Within a specification model, generalization means that the interface of the subtype must include all elements from the interface of the supertype. The subtype's interface is said to **conform to** the supertype's interface.

Another way of thinking of this involves the principle of **substitutability**. I should be able to substitute a Corporate Customer within any code that requires a Customer, and everything should work fine. Essentially, this means that if I write code assuming I have a Customer, I can freely use any subtype of Customer. The Corporate Customer may respond to certain commands differently from another Customer (using polymorphism), but the caller should not need to worry about the difference.

Generalization at the implementation perspective is associated with inheritance in programming languages. The subclass inherits all the methods and fields of the superclass and may override inherited methods.

The key point here is the difference between generalization at the specification perspective (subtyping, or interface-inheritance) and at the implementation perspective (subclassing, or implementation-inheritance). Subclassing is one way to implement subtyping. You can also implement subtyping through delegation—indeed, many of the patterns described in Gamma, Helm, Johnson, and Vlissides (1995) are about ways of having two classes with similar interfaces without using subclassing. You might also look at Fowler (1997) for other ideas on implementations for subtyping.

With either of these forms of generalization, you should always ensure that the conceptual generalization also applies. I have found that if you don't do this, you run into trouble because the generalization is not stable when you make changes later on.

Sometimes, you come across cases in which a subtype has the same interface as its supertype, but the subtype implements operations in a different way. If you do, you may choose not to show the subtype on a specification-perspective diagram. I usually do if the users of the class would find it of interest that subtypes may exist, but I don't if the subtypes are varied only because of internal implementation reasons.

Constraint Rules

Much of what you are doing in drawing a class diagram is indicating constraints.

Figure 4-2 indicates that an Order can be placed only by a single Customer. The diagram also implies that each Line Item is thought of separately: You say 40 brown widgets, 40 blue widgets, and 40 red widgets, not 40 red, blue, and brown widgets. Further, the diagram says that Corporate Customers have credit limits but Personal Customers do not.

The basic constructs of association, attribute, and generalization do much to specify important constraints, but they cannot indicate every constraint. These constraints still need to be captured; the class diagram is a good place to do that.

The UML allows you to use anything to describe constraints. The only rule is that you put them inside braces ({}). I like using informal English, emphasizing readability. The UML also provides a formal Object Constraint Language (OCL); see Warmer and Kleppe (1998).

Ideally, constraints should be implemented as assertions in your programming language. These correspond with the Design by Contract notion of invariants (see sidebar).

Design by Contract

Design by Contract is a design technique developed by Bertrand Meyer. The technique is a central feature of the Eiffel language he developed. Design by Contract is not specific to Eiffel, however; it is a valuable technique that can be used with any programming language.

At the heart of Design by Contract is the assertion. An **assertion** is a Boolean statement that should never be false and, therefore, will only be false because of a bug. Typically, assertions are checked only during debug and are not checked during production execution. Indeed, a program should never assume that assertions are being checked.

Design by Contract uses three kinds of assertions: post-conditions, pre-conditions, and invariants.

Pre-conditions and post-conditions apply to operations. A **post-condition** is a statement of what the world should look like after execution of an operation. For instance, if we define the operation "square root" on a number, the post-condition would take the form *input = result * result*, where *result* is the output and *input* is the input value. The post-condition is a useful way of saying what we do without saying how we do it—in other words, of separating interface from implementation.

A **pre-condition** is a statement of how we expect the world to be before we execute an operation. We might define a pre-condition for the "square root" operation of *input > = 0*. Such a pre-condition says that it is an error to invoke "square root" on a negative number and that the consequences of doing so are undefined.

On first glance, this seems a bad idea, because we should put some check somewhere to ensure that "square root" is invoked properly. The important question is who is responsible for doing so.

The pre-condition makes it explicit that the caller is responsible for checking. Without this explicit statement of responsibilities, we can get either too little checking (because both parties assume that the other is responsible) or too much (both parties check). Too much checking is a bad thing, because it leads to lots of duplicate checking code, which can significantly increase the complexity of a program. Being explicit about who is responsible helps to reduce this complexity. The danger that the caller forgets to check is reduced by the fact that assertions are usually checked during debugging and testing.

From these definitions of pre-condition and post-condition, we can see a strong definition of the term **exception**, which occurs when an operation is invoked with its pre-condition satisfied, yet it cannot return with its post-condition satisfied.

An **invariant** is an assertion about a class. For instance, an Account class may have an invariant that says that *balance == sum(entries.amount())*. The invariant is "always" true for all instances of the class. Here, "always" means "whenever the object is available to have an operation invoked on it."

In essence, this means that the invariant is added to pre-conditions and post-conditions associated with all public operations of the given class. The invariant may become false during execution of a method, but it should be restored to true by the time any other object can do anything to the receiver.

Assertions can play a unique role in subclassing.

One of the dangers of polymorphism is that you could redefine a subclass's operations to be inconsistent with the superclass's operations. Assertions stop you from doing this. The invariants and post-conditions of a class must apply to all subclasses. The subclasses can choose to strengthen these assertions, but they cannot weaken them. The pre-condition, on the other hand, cannot be strengthened but may be weakened.

This looks odd at first, but it is important to allow dynamic binding. You should always be able to treat a subclass object as if it were an instance of the superclass (per the principle of substitutability). If a subclass strengthened its pre-condition, then a superclass operation could fail when applied to the subclass.

Essentially, assertions can only increase the responsibilities of the subclass. Pre-conditions are a statement of passing a responsibility on to the caller; you increase the responsibilities of a class by weakening a pre-condition. In practice, all of this allows much better control of subclassing and helps you to ensure that subclasses behave properly.

Ideally, assertions should be included in the code as part of the interface definition. Compilers should be able to turn assertion checking on for debugging and remove it for production use. Various stages of assertion checking can be used. Pre-conditions often give you the best chances of catching errors for the least amount of processing overhead.

When to Use Design by Contract

Design by Contract is a valuable technique in building clear interfaces.

Only Eiffel supports assertions as part of its language, but Eiffel is, unfortunately, not a widely used language. It is straightforward, if awkward, to add mechanisms to other languages to support some assertions.

UML does not talk much about assertions, but you can use them without any trouble. Invariants are equivalent to constraint rules on class diagrams, and you should use these as much as possible. Operation pre-conditions and post-conditions should be documented within your operation definitions.

Where to Find Out More

Meyer's book (1997) is a classic (albeit now huge) work on OO design that talks a lot about assertions. Kim Walden and Jean-Marc Nerson (1995) and Steve Cook and John Daniels (1994) use Design by Contract extensively in their books.

You can also get more information from ISE (Bertrand Meyer's company) at **<www.eiffel.com>**.

When to Use Class Diagrams

Class diagrams are the backbone of nearly all OO methods, so you will find yourself using them all the time. This chapter covers the basic concepts; Chapter 6 discusses many of the advanced concepts.

The trouble with class diagrams is that they are so rich, they can be overwhelming to use. Here are a few tips.

- Don't try to use all the notations available to you. Start with the simple stuff in this chapter: classes, associations, attributes, generalization, and constraints. Introduce other notations from Chapter 6 only when you need them.

- Fit the perspective from which you are drawing the models to the stage of the project.

  — If you are in analysis, draw conceptual models.

  — When working with software, concentrate on specification models.

  — Draw implementation models only when you are illustrating a particular implementation technique.

- Don't draw models for everything; instead, concentrate on the key areas. It is better to have a few diagrams that you use and keep up to date than to have many forgotten, obsolete models.

The biggest danger with class diagrams is that you can get bogged down in implementation details far too early. To combat this, focus on the conceptual and specification perspectives. If you run into these problems, you may well find CRC cards (see page 75) to be extremely useful.

Where to Find Out More

All of the general UML books I mentioned in Chapter 1 talk about class diagrams in more detail.

Of the older books, I still like Cook and Daniels (1994) for its treatment of perspectives and the formality that the authors introduce.

Chapter 5

Interaction Diagrams

Interaction diagrams are models that describe how groups of objects collaborate in some behavior.

Typically, an interaction diagram captures the behavior of a single use case. The diagram shows a number of example objects and the messages that are passed between these objects within the use case.

I'll illustrate the approach with a simple use case that exhibits the following behavior.

- The Order Entry window sends a "prepare" message to an Order.
- The Order then sends "prepare" to each Order Line on the Order.
- Each Order Line checks the given Stock Item.
  - If this check returns "true," the Order Line removes the appropriate quantity of Stock Item from stock and creates a delivery item.
  - If the Stock Item has fallen below the reorder level, that Stock Item requests a reorder.

There are two kinds of interaction diagrams: sequence diagrams and collaboration diagrams.

Sequence Diagrams

Within a **sequence diagram**, an object is shown as a box at the top of a dashed vertical line (see Figure 5-1).

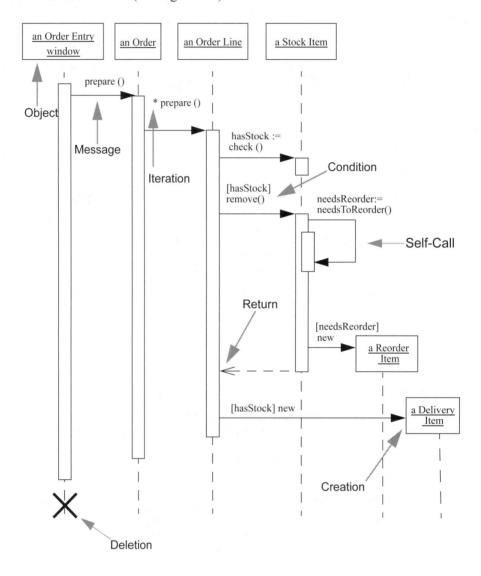

Figure 5-1: *Sequence Diagram*

This vertical line is called the object's **lifeline**. The lifeline represents the object's life during the interaction. This form was first popularized by Jacobson.

Each message is represented by an arrow between the lifelines of two objects. The order in which these messages occur is shown top to bottom on the page. Each message is labeled at minimum with the message name; you can also include the arguments and some control information. You can show a **self-call**, a message that an object sends to itself, by sending the message arrow back to the same lifeline.

To show when an object is active (for a procedural interaction, this would indicate that a procedure is on the stack), you include an activation box. You can omit activation boxes; this makes the diagrams easier to draw, but harder to understand.

Two bits of control information are valuable.

First, there is a **condition**, which indicates when a message is sent (for example, *[needsReorder]*). The message is sent only if the condition is true. Conditions are useful in simple cases like this, but for more complicated cases, I prefer to draw separate sequence diagrams for each case.

The second useful control marker is the **iteration marker**, which shows that a message is sent many times to multiple receiver objects, as would happen when you are iterating over a collection. You can show the basis of the iteration within brackets, such as *[for all order lines].

Figure 5-1 includes a **return**, which indicates a return from a message, not a new message. Returns differ from the regular messages in that the line is dashed. Some people draw a return for every message, but I find that clutters the diagram, so I draw them only when I feel they add clarity. The only reason I used a return in Figure 5-1 is to demonstrate the notation; if you remove the return, I think the diagram remains just as clear. That's a good test.

As you can see, Figure 5-1 is very simple and has immediate visual appeal. This is its great strength.

One of the hardest things to understand in an object-oriented program is the overall flow of control. A good design has lots of small methods in different classes, and at times it can be tricky to figure out the overall sequence of behavior. You can end up looking at the code trying to find the program. This is particularly true for those new to objects. Sequence diagrams help you to see that sequence.

Sequence diagrams are also valuable for concurrent processes.

In Figure 5-2, we see some objects that are checking a bank transaction.

When a Transaction is created, it creates a Transaction Coordinator to coordinate the checking of the Transaction. This coordinator creates a number (in this case, two) of Transaction Checker objects, each of which is responsible for a particular check. This process would make it easy to add different checking processes, because each checker is called asynchronously and proceeds in parallel.

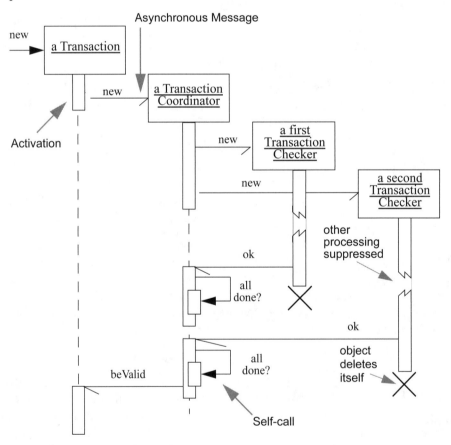

Figure 5-2: *Concurrent Processes and Activations*

When a Transaction Checker completes, it notifies the Transaction Coordinator. The coordinator looks to see whether all the checkers called back. If they haven't, the coordinator does nothing. If they have, and if all of them are successful, as in this case, the coordinator notifies the Transaction that all is well.

The half-arrowheads indicate an **asynchronous** message. An asynchronous message does not block the caller, so it can carry on with its own processing. An asynchronous message can do one of three things:

1. Create a new thread, in which case it links to the top of an activation
2. Create a new object
3. Communicate with a thread that is already running

Object **deletion** is shown with a large X. Objects can self-destruct (shown in Figure 5-2), or they can be destroyed by another message (see Figure 5-3).

Figure 5-2 and Figure 5-3 show two of the scenarios in the "transaction checking" use case. I have drawn each scenario separately. There are techniques for combining the conditional logic onto a single diagram, but I prefer not to use them, because it makes the diagram too complicated.

In Figure 5-3, I've employed a very useful technique: I've inserted textual descriptions of what's happening along the left side of the sequence diagram. This involves lining up each text block with the appropriate message within the diagram. This helps in understanding the diagram, albeit at the cost of some extra work. I do this for documents I'm going to keep but not for whiteboard sketches.

Collaboration Diagrams

The second form of the interaction diagram is the **collaboration diagram**.

Within a collaboration diagram, the example objects are shown as icons. As on a sequence diagram, arrows indicate the messages sent within the given use case. This time, however, the sequence is indicated by numbering the messages.

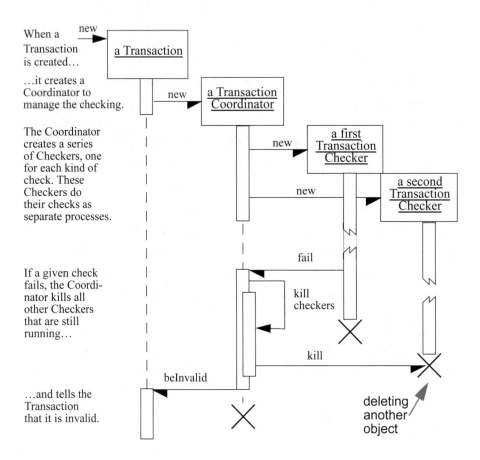

When a Transaction is created...

...it creates a Coordinator to manage the checking.

The Coordinator creates a series of Checkers, one for each kind of check. These Checkers do their checks as separate processes.

If a given check fails, the Coordinator kills all other Checkers that are still running...

...and tells the Transaction that it is invalid.

Figure 5-3: *Sequence Diagram: Check Failure*

Numbering the messages makes it more difficult to see the sequence than putting the lines down the page. On the other hand, the spatial layout allows you to show other things more easily. You can show how the objects are linked together and use the layout to overlay packages or other information.

You can use one of several numbering schemes for collaboration diagrams. The simplest is illustrated in Figure 5-4. Another approach involves a decimal numbering scheme, seen in Figure 5-5.

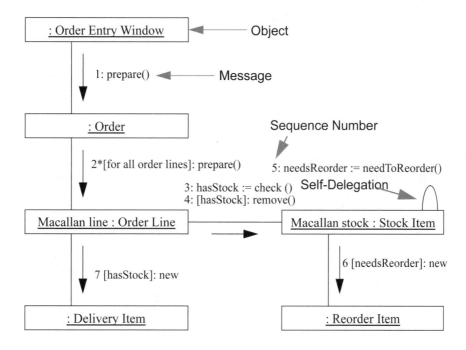

Figure 5-4: *Collaboration Diagram with Simple Numbering*

In the past, most people used the simple numbering scheme. The UML uses the decimal scheme because it makes it clear which operation is calling which other operation, although this makes it harder to see the overall sequence.

Regardless of what numbering scheme you use, you can add the same kind of control information you might show on a sequence diagram.

In Figure 5-4 and Figure 5-5, you can see the various forms of the UML's object naming scheme. This takes the form *objectName : ClassName*, where either the object name or the class name may be omitted. Note that if you omit the object name, you must retain the colon so that it is clear that it is the class name and not the object name. So the name "Macallan line : Order Line" indicates an instance of Order Line called Macallan line (this is an order I would particularly appreciate). I tend to name objects in the Smalltalk style that I used in the sequence diagrams. (This scheme is legal UML because "anObject" is a perfectly good name for an object.)

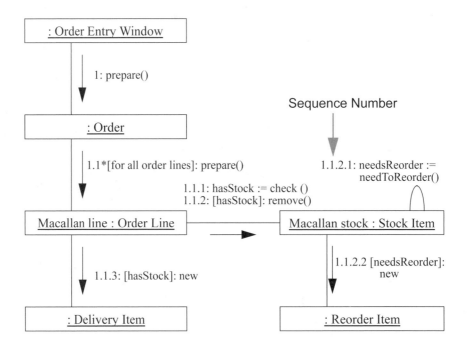

Figure 5-5: *Collaboration Diagram with Decimal Numbering*

Comparing Sequence and Collaboration Diagrams

Different developers have different preferences when it comes to choosing the form of interaction diagram to use. I usually prefer the sequence diagram because I like the emphasis it puts on sequence; it is easy to see the order in which things occur. Others prefer the collaboration diagram because they can use the layout to indicate how objects are statically connected.

One of the principal features of either form of an interaction diagram is its simplicity. You can easily see the messages by looking at the diagram. However, if you try to represent something other than a single sequential process without much conditional or looping behavior, the technique begins to break down.

One of the problems with interaction diagrams is that they can be awkward to use when exploring alternatives. Trying out alternatives leads to too much rubbing out and redrawing. As a result, I find CRC cards (see sidebar) very useful for exploring behavior.

CRC Cards

In the late 1980s, one the biggest centers of object technology was the research labs of Tektronix, in Portland, Oregon. These labs had some of the main users of Smalltalk, and many key ideas in object technology were developed there. Two renowned Smalltalk programmers there were Ward Cunningham and Kent Beck.

Cunningham and Beck were and are concerned about how to teach the deep knowledge of Smalltalk they had gained. From this question of how to teach objects came the simple technique of Class-Responsibility-Collaboration (CRC) cards.

Rather than use diagrams to develop models, as most methodologists did, Ward represented classes on 4 x 6 index cards. And rather than indicate attributes and methods on the cards, he wrote responsibilities.

So what is a responsibility? It is really a high-level description of the purpose of the class. The idea is to try to get away from a description of bits of data and process and instead capture the purpose of the class in a few sentences. The choice of a card is deliberate. You are not allowed to write more than will fit on the card (see Figure 5-6).

The second C refers to collaborators. These represent the other classes that this class needs to work with. This gives you some idea of the links between classes—still at a high level.

One of the chief benefits of CRC cards is that they encourage animated discussion among the developers. When you are working through a use case to see how classes will implement it, the interaction diagrams in this chapter can be slow to draw. Usually you need to consider alternatives, and with diagrams, the alternatives take too long to draw and rub out. With CRC cards, you model the interaction by picking up the cards and moving them around. This allows you to quickly consider alternatives.

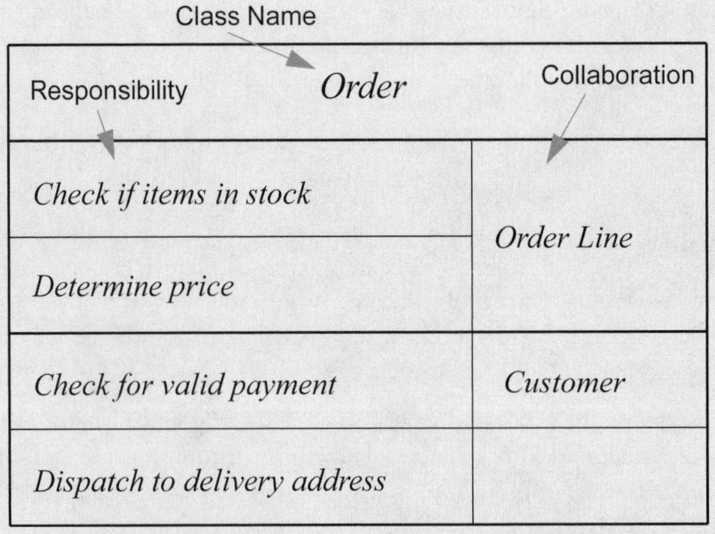

Class Name

Responsibility	*Order*	Collaboration
Check if items in stock		*Order Line*
Determine price		
Check for valid payment		*Customer*
Dispatch to delivery address		

Figure 5-6: *Class-Responsibility-Collaboration (CRC) Card*

As you do this, you form ideas about responsibilities and write them on the cards. Thinking about responsibilities is important, because it gets you away from classes as dumb data holders and eases the team members toward understanding the higher-level behavior of each class. A responsibility may correspond to an operation, to an attribute, or (more likely) to an undetermined clump of attributes and operations.

A common mistake I see people make is generating long lists of low-level responsibilities. This is really missing the point. The responsibilities should easily fit on a card. I would question any card with more than three responsibilities. Ask yourself whether the class should be split or whether the responsibilities would be better stated by rolling them up into higher-level statements.

When to Use CRC Cards

Use CRC cards to help explore an interaction between classes, typically to show how a scenario is implemented. Once you've figured out how the interaction works, you can document it with interaction diagrams.

Use responsibilities to help you summarize the key responsibilities of a class. They are useful in highlighting cluttered classes.

Many people stress the importance of role-playing, where each person on the team plays the role of one or more classes. I've never seen Ward or Kent do that, and I find it gets in the way.

Where to Find Out More

Sadly, Cunningham and Beck have never written a book about CRC, but you can find their original paper (Beck and Cunningham 1989) on the Web (<**http://c2.com/doc/oopsla89/paper. html**>). On the whole, the book that best describes this technique—and, indeed, the whole notion of using responsibilities—is Wirfs-Brock (1990). It is a relatively old book by OO standards, but it has aged well.

When to Use Interaction Diagrams

You should use interaction diagrams when you want to look at the behavior of several objects within a single use case. Interaction diagrams are good at showing collaborations among the objects; they are not so good at precise definition of the behavior.

If you want to look at the behavior of a single object across many use cases, use a state diagram (see Chapter 8). If you want to look at behavior across many use cases or many threads, consider an activity diagram (see Chapter 9).

Chapter 6

Class Diagrams: Advanced Concepts

The concepts described in Chapter 4 correspond to the key notations in class diagrams. Those concepts are the first ones to understand and become familiar with, as they will comprise 90 percent of your effort in building class diagrams.

The class diagram technique, however, has bred dozens of notations for additional concepts. I find that I don't use these all the time, but they are handy when they are appropriate. I'll discuss them one at a time and point out some of the issues in using them. Remember, however, that they are all optional, and many people have got a lot of value out of class diagrams without using these additional items.

You'll probably find this chapter somewhat heavy going. The good news is that during your first pass through the book, you can safely skip this chapter and come back to it later.

Stereotypes

Stereotypes are the core extension mechanism of the UML. If you find that you need a modeling construct that isn't in the UML but is similar to something that is, you treat your construct as a stereotype of the UML construct.

An example of this is the interface. A UML **interface** is a class that has only public operations with no method bodies or attributes. This corresponds to interfaces in Java, COM, and CORBA. Since it's a special kind of class, it is defined as a stereotype of class. (See "Interfaces and Abstract Classes" on page 89 for more about interfaces.)

Stereotypes are usually shown in text between guillemets (for example, «interface»), but you can also show them by defining an icon for the stereotype.

Many extensions to the core UML can be described as a collection of stereotypes. Within class diagrams, these might be stereotypes of classes, associations, or generalizations. You can think of the stereotypes as subtypes of the metamodel types Class, Association, and Generalization.

I've noticed that people using the UML tend to confuse constraints and stereotypes. If you mark a class as abstract, is that a constraint or a stereotype? The current official documents call it a constraint, but you should be aware that there is a blurred usage between the two. This is not surprising, as subtypes are often more constrained than supertypes.

UML 1.4 introduced profiles. A **profile** takes a part of the UML and extends it with a coherent group of stereotypes for a particular purpose, such as business modeling.

Object Diagram

An **object diagram** is a snapshot of the objects in a system at a point in time. Since it shows instances rather than classes, an object diagram is often called an instance diagram.

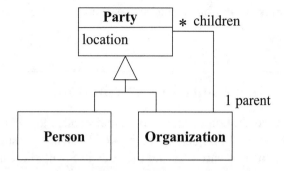

Figure 6-1: *Class Diagram of Party Composition Structure*

You can use an instance diagram to show an example configuration of objects. (See Figure 6-1, which shows a set of classes, and Figure 6-2, which shows an associated set of objects.) This is very useful when the possible connections between objects are complicated.

You can tell that the elements in Figure 6-2 are instances because the names are underlined. Each name takes the form *instance name : class name*. Both parts of the name are optional, so John and :Person are legal names. You can then show values for attributes and links, as in Figure 6-2.

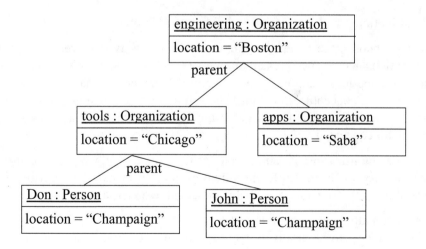

Figure 6-2: *Object Diagram Showing Example Instances of* **Party**

You can also think of an object diagram as a collaboration diagram without messages.

Class Scope Operations and Attributes

UML refers to an operation or an attribute that applies to a class, rather than an instance, as having **class scope**. This is equivalent to static members in C++ or Java and to class variables and methods in Smalltalk. Class scope features are <u>underlined</u> on a class diagram (see Figure 6-3).

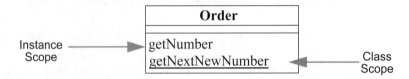

Figure 6-3: *Class Scope Notation*

Multiple and Dynamic Classification

Classification refers to the relationship between an object and its type.

Most methods make certain assumptions about this type of relationship— assumptions that are also present in mainstream OO programming languages. These assumptions were questioned by Jim Odell, who felt that they were too restrictive for conceptual modeling. The assumptions are of single, static classification of objects; Odell suggests using multiple, dynamic classification of objects for conceptual models.

In **single classification**, an object belongs to a single type, which may inherit from supertypes. In **multiple classification**, an object may be described by several types that are not necessarily connected by inheritance.

Note that multiple classification is different from multiple inheritance. Multiple inheritance says that a type may have many supertypes, but that a single type must be defined for each object. Multiple classification allows multiple types for an object without defining a specific type for the purpose.

For example, consider a person subtyped as either man or woman, doctor or nurse, patient or not (see Figure 6-4). Multiple classification allows an object to have any of these types assigned to it in any allowable combination, without the need for types to be defined for all the legal combinations.

If you use multiple classification, you need to be sure that you make it clear which combinations are legal. You do this by labeling a generalization line with a **discriminator**, which is an indication of the basis of the subtyping. Several subtypes can share the same discriminator. All subtypes with the same discriminator are disjoint; that is, any instance of the supertype may be an instance of only one of the subtypes within that discriminator. A good convention is to have all subclasses that use one discriminator roll up to one triangle, as shown in Figure 6-4. Alternatively, you can have several arrows with the same text label.

A useful constraint is to say that any instance of the superclass must be an instance of one of the subtypes of a group. (The superclass is then abstract.) There's some confusion in the standard at the moment, but many people use the constraint {complete} to show this.

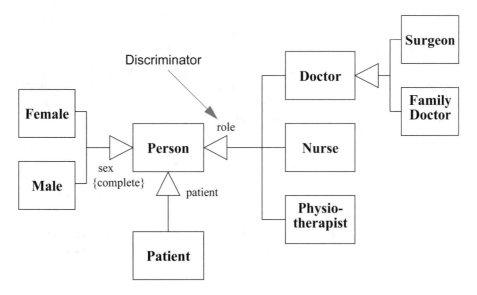

Figure 6-4: *Multiple Classification*

To illustrate, note the following legal combinations of subtypes in the diagram: (Female, Patient, Nurse); (Male, Physiotherapist); (Female, Patient); and (Female, Doctor, Surgeon). Note also that such combinations as (Patient, Doctor) and (Male, Doctor, Nurse) are illegal. The first set is illegal because it doesn't include a type from the {complete} Sex discriminator; the second set is illegal because it contains two types from the Role discriminator. Single classification, by definition, corresponds to a single, unlabeled discriminator.

Another question is whether an object may change its type. For example, when a bank account is overdrawn, it substantially changes its behavior. Specifically, several operations (including "withdraw" and "close") get overridden.

Dynamic classification allows objects to change type within the subtyping structure; **static classification** does not. With static classification, a separation is made between types and states; dynamic classification combines these notions.

Should you use multiple, dynamic classification? I believe it is useful for conceptual modeling. You can do it with specification modeling, but you have to be comfortable with the techniques for implementing it. The trick is to implement in such a way that it looks the same as subclassing from the interface so that a user of a class cannot tell which implementation is being used. (See Fowler 1997 for some techniques.) However, like most of these things, the choice depends on the circumstances, and you have to use your best judgment. The transformation from a multiple, dynamic interface to a single static implementation may well be more trouble than it is worth.

Figure 6-5 shows an example of using dynamic classification for a person's job, which, of course, can change. This can be appropriate, but the subtypes would need additional behavior, instead of being just labels. In these cases, it is often worth creating a separate class for the job and linking the person to it with an association. I wrote a pattern, called *Role Models*, on this subject; you can find information about this pattern, and other information that supplements my *Analysis Patterns* book, on my home page.

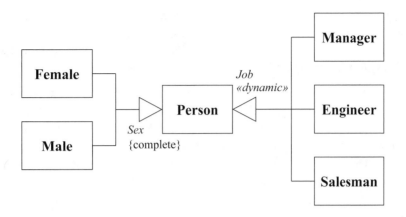

Figure 6-5: *Dynamic Classification*

Aggregation and Composition

One of my biggest *bêtes noire*s in modeling is aggregation. It's easy to explain glibly: **Aggregation** is the part-of relationship. It's like saying that a car has an engine and wheels as its parts. This sounds good, but the difficult thing is considering what the difference is between aggregation and association.

In the pre-UML days, people were usually rather vague on what was aggregation and what was association. Whether vague or not, they were always inconsistent with everyone else. As a result, many modelers think that aggregation is important, although for different reasons. So the UML included aggregation, but with hardly any semantics. As Jim Rumbaugh says, "Think of it as a modeling placebo" (Rumbaugh, Jacobson, and Booch 1999).

In addition to aggregation, the UML offers a stronger variety of aggregation, called composition. With **composition**, the part object may belong to only one whole; further, the parts are usually expected to live and die with the whole. Usually, any deletion of the whole is considered to cascade to the parts.

This cascading delete is often considered to be a defining part of aggregation, but it is implied by any association end with a 1..1 multiplicity; if you really want to delete a Customer, for instance, you must cascade that delete to Orders (and thus to Order Lines).

Figure 6-6 shows examples of these constructs. The compositions to *Point* indicate that any instance of *Point* may be in either a *Polygon* or a *Circle*, but not both. An instance of *Style*, however, may be shared by many *Polygon*s and *Circle*s. Furthermore, this implies that deleting a *Polygon* would cause its associated *Point*s to be deleted, but *not* the associated *Style*.

This constraint—that a *Point* may appear in only one *Polygon* or *Circle* at a time—could not be expressed by the multiplicities alone. It also implies that the point is a value object (see "Reference Objects and Value Objects" on page 92). You can add a 0..1 multiplicity to a composite side of the association, but often I don't bother. The black diamond says all that needs to be said.

Figure 6-7 shows another notation for composition. In this case, you put the component inside the whole. The component class's name is not bold, and you write it in the form *rolename:Class name*. In addition, you put the multiplicity in the top right corner. You can also use an attribute for a single-valued component.

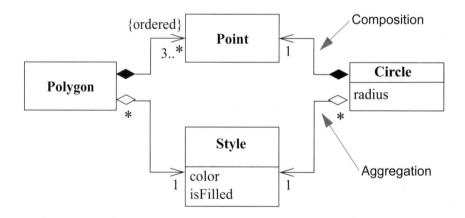

Figure 6-6: *Aggregation and Composition*

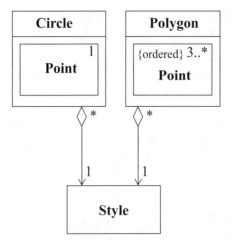

Figure 6-7: *Alternative Notation for Composition*

Different composition notations work for different situations. There are a couple more, although the variety of composition notations offered by the UML does get rather overwhelming. Note that these variations can be used only for composition, not aggregation.

Derived Associations and Attributes

Derived associations and **derived attributes** can be calculated from other associations and attributes, respectively, on a class diagram. For example, an age attribute of a Person can be derived if you know that Person's date of birth.

Each perspective brings its own interpretation of derived features on class diagrams. The most critical of these has to do with the specification perspective. From this angle, it is important to realize that derived features indicate a constraint between values, not a statement of what is calculated and what is stored.

Figure 6-8 shows a hierarchical structure of accounts drawn from a specification perspective. The model uses the *Composite* pattern (see Gamma, Helm, Johnson, and Vlissides 1995).

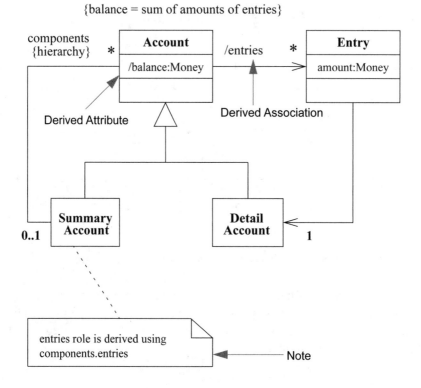

Figure 6-8: *Derived Associations and Attributes*

Note the following.

- Entry objects are attached to Detail Accounts.
- The balance of an Account is calculated as the sum of Entry amounts.
- A Summary Account's entries are the entries of its components, determined recursively.

Since Figure 6-8 illustrates a specification model, it does not state that Accounts do not contain fields to hold balances; such a cache may well be present, but it is hidden from the clients of the Account class.

I can illustrate how derived elements indicate constraints with a class named Time Period (see Figure 6-9).

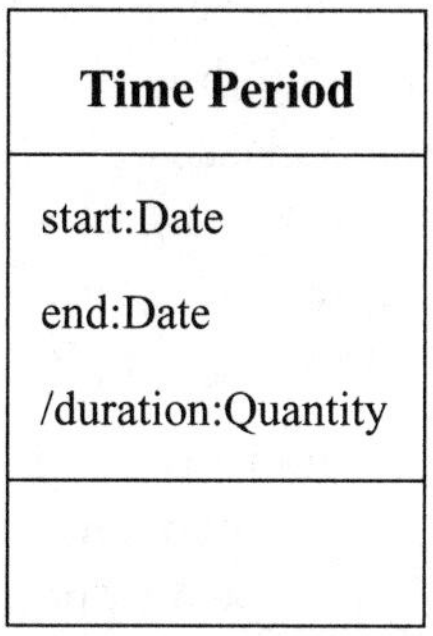

Time Period
start:Date
end:Date
/duration:Quantity

Figure 6-9: *Time Period Class*

If this is a specification diagram, although it suggests that *start* and *end* are stored and that *duration* is calculated, a programmer can, in fact, implement this class in any fashion that maintains that external behavior. For instance, storing *start* and *duration* and calculating *end* is perfectly acceptable.

On implementation diagrams, derived values are valuable for annotating fields that are used as caches for performance reasons. By marking them and recording the derivation of the cache, it is easier to see explicitly what the cache is doing. I often reinforce this in the code by using the word "cache" on the name (for instance, *balanceCache*).

On conceptual diagrams, I use derived markers to remind me where these derivations exist and to confirm with the domain experts that the derivations exist. They then correlate with their use in specification diagrams.

Interfaces and Abstract Classes

One of the great qualities of object-oriented development is that you can vary the interfaces of classes independent of the implementation. Much of the power of object development comes from this property. However, few people make good use of it.

Programming languages use a single construct, the class, which contains both interface and implementation. When you subclass, you inherit both. Using the interface as a separate construct is rarely used, which is a shame.

A pure interface, as in Java, is a class with no implementation and, therefore, has operation declarations but no method bodies and no fields. Interfaces are often declared through abstract classes. Such classes may provide some implementation, but often they are used primarily to declare an interface. The point is that subclassing—or some other mechanism—will provide the implementation, but clients will never see the implementation, only the interface.

The text editor represented in Figure 6-10 is a typical example of this. To allow the editor to be platform-independent, we define a platform-independent abstract Window class. This class has no method bodies; it only defines an interface for the text editor to use. Platform-specific subclasses can be used as desired.

If you have an abstract class or method, the UML convention is to italicize the name of the abstract item. You can use the {abstract} constraint, as well (or instead). I use {abstract} on whiteboards because I can't write italic text. With a diagramming tool, however, I prefer the elegance of italics.

Subclassing is not the only way to do this, however. Java provides an interface construct, and the compiler checks that the implementing class provides implementations of all of the interface's operations.

In Figure 6-11, we see InputStream, DataInput, and DataInputStream (defined in the standard *java.io* package). InputStream is an abstract class; DataInput is an interface.

Some client class, say, OrderReader, needs to use DataInput's functionality. The DataInputStream class implements both the DataInput and InputStream interfaces and is a subclass of the latter.

The link between DataInputStream and DataInput is a **realization** relationship. Realization is deliberately similar to generalization; it indicates that one class implements behavior specified by another. It is permissible for one implementation class to realize another; this means that the realizing class must conform to the interface, but need not use inheritance.

In a specification model, there is no difference between realization and subtyping.

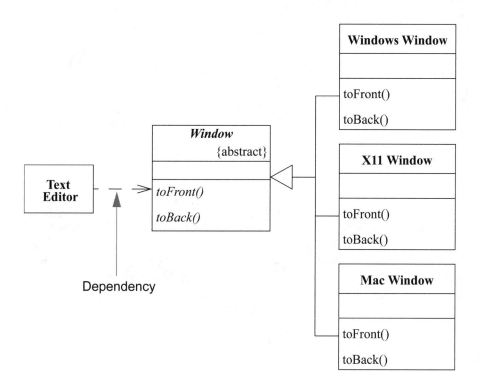

Figure 6-10: *Window as Abstract Class*

The link between OrderReader and DataInput is a **dependency**. In this case, the dependency indicates that if the DataInput interface changes, the Order-Reader may also have to change. One of the aims of development is to keep dependencies to a minimum so that the effects of changes are minimized. (There's more on dependencies in Chapter 7.)

Figure 6-12 shows an alternative, more compact notation. Here, the interfaces are represented by small circles (often called lollipops) coming off the classes that implement them.

With lollipops, there is no distinction between realizing an interface and sub-classing an abstract class. Although the notation is more compact, you cannot show the operations of the interface or any generalization relationships between interfaces.

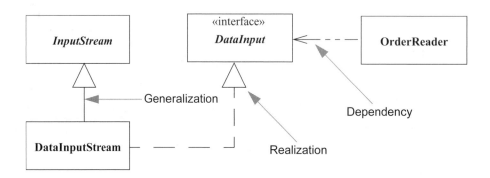

Figure 6-11: *Interfaces and Abstract Class: An Example from Java*

Abstract classes and interfaces are similar, but there is a difference. Both allow you to define an interface and defer its implementation until later. However, the abstract class allows you to add implementation of some of the methods; an interface forces you to defer definition of all methods.

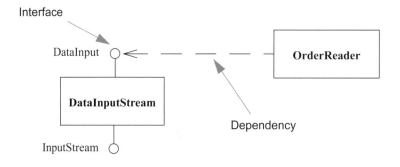

Figure 6-12: *Lollipop Notation for Interfaces*

Reference Objects and Value Objects

One of the common things said about objects is that they have identity. This is true, but it is not quite as simple as that. In practice, you find that identity is important for reference objects, but not so important for value objects.

Reference objects are things like Customer. Here, identity is very important, because you usually want only one software object to designate a customer in the real world. Any object that references a Customer object will do so through a reference or pointer; all objects that reference this Customer will reference the same software object. That way, changes to a Customer are available to all users of the Customer.

If you have two references to a Customer and you wish to see whether they are the same, you usually compare their identities. Copies may be disallowed; if they are allowed, they tend to be made rarely, perhaps for archive purposes or for replication across a network. If copies are made, you need to sort out how to synchronize changes.

Value objects are things like Date. You often have multiple value objects representing the same object in the real world. For example, it is normal to have hundreds of objects that designate 1-Jan-99. These are all interchangeable copies. New dates are created and destroyed frequently.

If you have two dates and you wish to see whether they are the same, you don't look at their identities, but rather at the values they represent. This usually means that you have to write an equality test operator, which for dates would make a test on year, month, and day (or whatever the internal representation is). Usually each object that references 1-Jan-99 has its own dedicated object, but you can also share dates.

Value objects should be immutable (frozen; see "Frozen" on page 94). In other words, you should not be able to take a date object of 1-Jan-99 and change the same date object to be 2-Jan-99. Instead, you should create a new 2-Jan-99 object and link to that first object. The reason is that if the date were shared, you would update another object's date in an unpredictable way.

In days gone by, the difference between reference objects and value objects was clearer. Value objects were the built-in values of the type system. Now you can extend the type system with your own classes, so this issue requires more thought. Within the UML, attributes are usually used for value objects, and associations are used for reference objects. You can also use composition for value objects.

I don't find that the distinction between reference and value objects is useful with conceptual models. It can cause confusion with multiplicities. If I represent a link to a value object with an association, I usually mark the multiplicity of the end on the user of the given value as *, unless there is a uniqueness rule, such as a sequence number.

Collections for Multivalued Association Ends

A **multivalued end** is one whose multiplicity's upper bound is greater than 1 (for instance, *). The usual convention is that multivalued ends are thought of as sets. There is no ordering for the target objects, and no object appears in the set more than once. You can change these assumptions, however, by attaching a constraint.

The *{ordered}* constraint implies that there is an ordering to the target objects—that is, the target objects form a list. Target objects may appear only once in the list.

I use the *{bag}* constraint to indicate that target objects may appear more than once, but there is no ordering. I also use the *{hierarchy}* constraint to indicate that the target objects form a hierarchy, and I use the *{dag}* constraint to indicate a directed acyclic graph.

Frozen

Frozen is a constraint that the UML defines as applicable to an attribute or an association end, but I find it useful for classes as well.

On an attribute or association end, frozen indicates that the value of that attribute or association end may not change during the lifetime of the source object. The value must be set at object creation and may never change after that. The initial value may be null. Of course, if that's true when the object is constructed, it will be true as long as the object is alive. This implies that there is usually an argument for this value in a constructor and that there is no operation that updates this value.

When applied to a class, frozen indicates that all association ends and attributes associated with that class are frozen.

Frozen is *not* the same as read-only. Read-only implies that a value cannot be changed directly but may change due to a change in some other value. For instance, if a person has a date of birth and an age, the age may be read-only, but it cannot be frozen.

I mark "freezing" using the *{frozen}* constraint, and I mark read-only values with *{read only}*. (Note that Read Only is not a standard UML property.)

If you are thinking of "freezing" something, bear in mind that people make mistakes. In software, we model what we know about the world, not how the world is. If we were modeling how the world is, a "date of birth" attribute for a Person object would be frozen, but for most cases, we would want to change it if we found that a previous recording was incorrect.

Classification and Generalization

I often hear people talk about subtyping as the "is a" relationship. I urge you to beware of that way of thinking. The problem is that the phrase "is a" can mean different things.

Consider the following phrases.

1. Shep is a Border Collie.
2. A Border Collie is a Dog.
3. Dogs are Animals.
4. A Border Collie is a Breed.
5. Dog is a Species.

Now try combining the phrases. If I combine phrases 1 and 2, I get "Shep is a Dog"; 2 and 3 taken together yield "Border Collies are Animals." And 1 plus 2 plus 3 gives me "Shep is an Animal." So far, so good. Now try 1 and 4: "Shep is a Breed." The combination of 2 and 5 is "A Border Collie is a Species." These are not so good.

Why can I combine some of these phrases and not others? The reason is that some are **classification** (the object Shep is an instance of the type Border Collie), and some are **generalization** (the type Border Collie is a subtype of the type Dog). Generalization is transitive; classification is not. I can combine a classification followed by a generalization, but not vice versa.

Figure 6-13: *Qualified Association*

I make this point to get you to be wary of "is a." Using it can lead to inappropriate use of subclassing and confused responsibilities. Better tests for subtyping in this case would be the phrases "Dogs are kinds of Animals" and "Every instance of a Border Collie is an instance of a Dog."

Qualified Associations

A **qualified association** is the UML equivalent of a programming concept variously known as associative arrays, maps, and dictionaries.

Figure 6-13 shows a way of representing the association between the Order and Order Line classes that uses a qualifier. The qualifier says that in connection with an Order, there may be one Order Line for each instance of Product.

Conceptually, this example indicates that you cannot have two Order Lines within an Order for the same Product. From a specification perspective, this qualified association would imply an interface along the lines of

```
class Order {

    public OrderLine getLineItem
        (Product aProduct);

    public void addLineItem
        (Number amount, Product forProduct);
```

Thus, all access to a given Line Item requires a Product as an argument. A multiplicity of 1 would indicate that there must be a Line Item for every Product; * would indicate that you can have multiple Order Lines per Product but that access to the Line Items is still indexed by Product.

From an implementation perspective, this suggests the use of an associative array or similar data structure to hold the order lines.

```
Class Order {

    private Map _lineItems;
```

In conceptual modeling, I use the qualifier construct only to show constraints along the lines of "single Order Line per Product on Order." In specification models, I use it to show a keyed lookup interface. I'm quite happy to use both this and an unqualified association at the same time if that is a suitable interface.

I use qualifiers within implementation models to show uses of a map, dictionary, associative array, or similar data structure.

Association Class

Association classes allow you to add attributes, operations, and other features to associations, as shown in Figure 6-14.

We can see from the diagram that a Person may work for a single Company. We need to keep information about the period of time that each employee works for each Company.

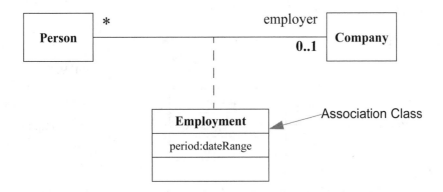

Figure 6-14: *Association Class*

We can do this by adding a *dateRange* attribute to the association. We could add this attribute to the Person class, but it is really a fact about a Person's relationship to a Company, which will change should the person's employer change.

Figure 6-15 shows another way to represent this information: make Employment a full class in its own right. (Note how the multiplicities have been moved accordingly.) In this case, each of the classes in the original association has a single-valued association end with regard to the Employment class. The "employer" end now is derived, although you don't have to show this.

What benefit do you gain with the association class to offset the extra notation you have to remember? The association class adds an extra constraint, in that there can be only one instance of the association class between any two participating objects. I feel the need for an example.

Take a look at the two diagrams in Figure 6-16. These diagrams have much the same form. However, we could imagine a Person working for the same Company at different periods of time—that is, he or she leaves and later returns. This means that a Person could have more than one Employment association with the same Company over time. With regard to the Person and Skill classes, it would be hard to see why a Person would have more than one Competency in the same Skill; indeed, you would probably consider that an error.

In the UML, only the latter case is legal. You can have only one Competency for each combination of Person and Skill.

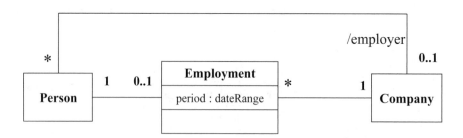

Figure 6-15: *Promoting an Association Class to a Full Class*

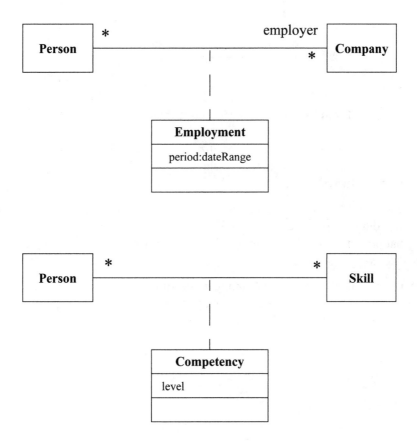

Figure 6-16: *Association Class Subtleties*

The top diagram in Figure 6-16 would not allow a Person to have more than one Employment with the same Company. If you need to allow this, you need to make Employment a full class, in the style of Figure 6-15.

In the past, modelers made various assumptions about the meaning of an association class in these circumstances. Some assumed that you can have only unique combinations, such as competency, whereas others did not assume such a constraint.

Figure 6-17: *History Stereotype for Associations*

Many people did not think about it at all and may have assumed the constraint in some places and not in others. So when using the UML, remember that the constraint is always there.

You often find this kind of construct with historical information, such as in the preceding Employment case. A useful pattern here is the *Historic Mapping* pattern described in Fowler (1997). We can use this by defining a «history» stereotype (see Figure 6-17).

The model indicates that a Person may work for only a single Company at one time. Over time, however, a Person may work for several Companies. This suggests an interface along the lines of

```
class Person {

  //get current employer
  Company getEmployer();

  //employer at a given date
  Company getEmployer(Date);

  void changeEmployer(Company newEmployer,
     Date changeDate);

  void leaveEmployer (Date changeDate);
```

The «history» stereotype is not part of the UML, but I mention it here for two reasons. First, it is a notion I have found useful on several occasions in my modeling career. Second, it shows how you can use stereotypes to extend the UML. You can read a lot more about this at <**http://martinfowler.com/ap2/timeNarrative.html**>.

Parameterized Class

Several languages, most noticeably C++, have the notion of a **parameterized class**, or **template**.

This concept is most obviously useful for working with collections in a strongly typed language. This way, you can define behavior for sets in general by defining a template class Set.

```
class Set <T> {
    void insert (T newElement);
    void remove (T anElement);
```

When you have done this, you can use the general definition to make set classes for more specific elements.

```
    Set <Employee> employeeSet;
```

You declare a parameterized class in the UML using the notation shown in Figure 6-18.

The T in the diagram is a placeholder for the type parameter. (You may have more than one.) In an untyped language, such as Smalltalk, this issue does not come up, so this concept is not useful.

A use of a parameterized class, such as *Set<Employee>*, is called a **bound element**.

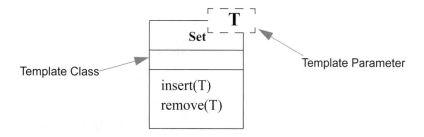

Figure 6-18: *Parameterized Class*

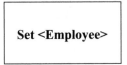

Figure 6-19: *Bound Element (Version 1)*

You can show a bound element in two ways. The first way mirrors the C++ syntax (see Figure 6-19).

The alternative notation (see Figure 6-20) reinforces the link to the template and allows you to rename the bound element.

The «bind» stereotype is a stereotype on the refinement relationship. This relationship indicates that EmployeeSet will conform to the interface of Set. In specification terms, the EmployeeSet is a subtype of Set. This fits the other way of implementing type-specific collections, which is to declare all appropriate subtypes.

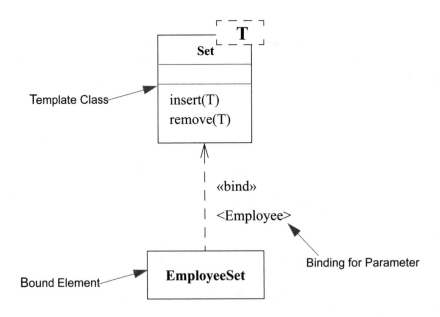

Figure 6-20: *Bound Element (Version 2)*

Using a bound element is *not* the same as subtyping, however. You are not allowed to add features to the bound element, which is completely specified by its template; you are adding only restricting type information. If you want to add features, you must create a subtype.

Parameterized classes allow you to use a derived typing. When you write the body of the template, you may invoke operations on the parameter. When you later declare a bound element, the compiler tries to ensure that the supplied parameter supports the operations required by the template.

This is a derived typing mechanism because you do not have to define a type for the parameter; the compiler figures out whether the binding is viable, by looking at the source of the template. This property is central to the use of parameterized classes in C++'s standard template library (STL); these classes can also be used for other interesting tricks.

Using parameterized classes does have repercussions—for example, they can cause considerable code bloat in C++. I rarely use parameterized classes in conceptual modeling, mostly because they are used mainly for collections, which are implied by associations. (One case I do use it for is the *Range* pattern; see Fowler 1997). I use parameterized classes in specification and implementation modeling only if they are supported by the language I am using.

Visibility

I must confess to having some trepidation about this section.

Visibility is one of those subjects that is simple in principle but has complex subtleties. The simple idea is that any class has public and private elements. Public elements can be used by any other class; private elements can be used only by the owning class. However, each language makes its own rules. Although many languages use terms such as "public," "private," and "protected," they mean different things in different languages. These differences are small, but they lead to confusion, especially for those of us who use more than one language.

The UML tries to address this without getting into a horrible tangle. Essentially, within the UML, you can tag any attribute or operation with a visibility indicator. You can use any marker you like, and its meaning is language-dependent. However, the UML provides four (rather hard to remember) abbreviations for visibility: + (public), – (private), ~ (package) and # (protected).

I'm tempted to leave it at that, but unfortunately, people draw diagrams that use visibility in specific ways. Therefore, to really understand some of the common differences that exist among models, you need to understand the approaches that different languages take to visibility. So, let's take a deep breath and dive into the murk.

We start with C++, because it's the basis for standard UML usage.

- A public member is visible anywhere in the program and may be called by any object within the system.
- A private member may be used only by the class that defines it.
- A protected member may be used only by (a) the class that defines it or (b) a subclass of that class.

Consider a Customer class that has a Personal Customer subclass. Consider also the object Martin, which is an instance of Personal Customer. Martin can use any public member of any object in the system. Martin may also use any private member of the class Personal Customer. Martin may *not* use any private members defined within Customer; Martin may, however, use protected members of Customer and protected members of Personal Customer.

Now look at Smalltalk. Within that language, all instance variables are private, and all operations are public. However, private doesn't mean the same thing in Smalltalk that it does in C++. In a Smalltalk system, Martin can access any instance variable within his own object whether that instance variable was defined within Customer or Personal Customer. So, in a sense, private in Smalltalk is similar to protected in C++.

Ah, but that would be too simple.

Let's go back to C++. Say that I have another instance of Personal Customer, called Kendall. Kendall can access any member of Martin that was defined as part of the Personal Customer class, whether public, private, or protected. Kendall may also access any protected or public member of Martin that was defined within Customer. However, in Smalltalk, Kendall cannot access Martin's private instance variables—only Martin's public operations.

In C++, you may access members of other objects of your own class in the same way that you access your own members. In Smalltalk, it makes no difference whether another object is of the same class or not; you can access only public parts of another object.

Java is similar to C++ in that it offers free access to members of other objects of one's own class. Java also adds a new visibility level, called package. A member with package visibility may be accessed only by instances of other classes within the same package.

In keeping with our theme, to ensure that things are not too simple, Java slightly redefines protected visibility. In Java, a protected member may be accessed by subclasses but also by any other class in the same package as the owning class. This means that in Java, protected is more public than package.

Java also allows classes to be marked public or package. A public class's public members may be used by any class that imports the package to which the class belongs. A package class may be used only by other classes in the same package.

C++ adds a final twist. One C++ method or class can be made a friend of a class. A **friend** has complete access to all members of a class—hence, the phrase "in C++, friends touch each other's private parts."

When you are using visibility, use the rules of the language in which you are working. When you are looking at a UML model from elsewhere, be wary of the meanings of the visibility markers, and be aware of how those meanings can change from language to language.

I usually find that visibilities change as you work with the code. So, don't get too hung up on them early on.

Chapter 7

Packages and Collaborations

One of the oldest questions in software methods is: How do you break down a large system into smaller systems? We ask this question because as systems get large, it becomes difficult to understand them and the changes we make to them.

Structured methods used **functional decomposition**, in which the overall system was mapped as a function and broken down into sub-functions, which were broken down further into sub-sub-functions, and so forth. The functions were like the use cases in an object-oriented system in that functions represented something the system as a whole did.

Those were the days when process and data were separated. So in addition to a functional decomposition, there was also a data structure. This took second place, although some Information Engineering techniques grouped data records into subject areas and produced matrices to show how the functions and data records interacted.

It is from this viewpoint that we see the biggest change that objects have wrought. The separation of process and data is gone, and functional decomposition is gone, but the old question still remains.

One idea is to group the classes together into higher-level units. This idea, applied very loosely, appears in many object methods. In the UML, this grouping mechanism is called the **package**.

Packages

The idea of a package can be applied to any model element, not just classes. Without some heuristics to group classes together, the grouping becomes arbitrary. The one I have found most useful and the one stressed most in the UML is the dependency.

I use the term **package diagram** for a diagram that shows packages of classes and the dependencies among them. Strictly speaking, a package diagram is just a class diagram that shows only packages and dependencies. I use these diagrams quite a lot, so I name them package diagrams, but you should remember that that is my term, not an official UML diagram name.

A **dependency** exists between two elements if changes to the definition of one element may cause changes to the other. With classes, dependencies exist for various reasons: One class sends a message to another; one class has another as part of its data; one class mentions another as a parameter to an operation. If a class changes its interface, any message sent to it may no longer be valid.

Ideally, only changes to a class's interface should affect any other class. The art of large-scale design involves minimizing dependencies; that way, the effects of change are reduced, and the system requires less effort to change.

The UML has many varieties of dependency, each with particular semantics and stereotype. I find it easier to begin with the unstereotyped dependency and use the more particular dependencies only if I need to.

In Figure 7-1, we have domain classes that model the business, grouped into two packages: Orders and Customers. Both packages are part of an overall domain package. The Order Capture application has dependencies with both domain packages. The Order Capture UI has dependencies with the Order Capture application and the AWT (a Java GUI toolkit).

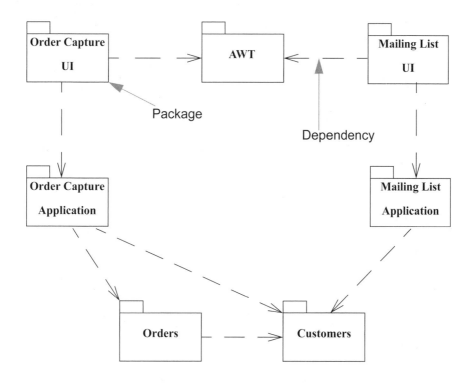

Figure 7-1: *Package Diagram*

A dependency between two packages exists if any dependency exists between any two classes in the packages. For example, if any class in the Mailing List package is dependent on any class in the Customers package, a dependency exists between their corresponding packages.

There is an obvious similarity between these dependencies and compilation dependencies. In fact, there is a vital difference: With packages, the dependencies are not transitive.

An example of a **transitive** relationship is one in which Jim has a larger beard than Grady, and Grady has a larger beard than Ivar, so we can deduce that Jim has a larger beard than Ivar.

To see why this is important for dependencies, look at Figure 7-1 again. If a class in the Orders package changes, this does not indicate that the Order Capture UI package needs to be changed. It merely indicates that the Order Capture application package needs to be looked at to see if it changes. Only if the

Order Capture application package's interface is altered does the Order Capture UI package need to change. In this case, the Order Capture application is shielding the Order Capture UI from changes to orders.

This behavior is the classic purpose of a layered architecture. Indeed, these are similar to the semantics of the Java "imports" behavior but not that of the C/C++ "includes" behavior. The C/C++ includes is transitive, which means that the Order Capture UI would be dependent on the Orders package. A transitive dependency makes it difficult to limit the scope of changes with compilation. (Although most dependencies are not transitive, you can create a particular stereotyped dependency that is.)

Classes within packages can be public, private, or protected. So, the Orders package is dependent on the public methods of the public classes in the Customers package. If you alter a private method, or a public method on a private class, in the Customers package, none of the classes in the Orders package needs to change.

A useful technique here is to reduce the interface of the package by exporting only a small subset of the operations associated with the package's public classes. You can do this by giving all classes private visibility, so that they can be seen only by other classes in the same package, and by adding extra public classes for the public behavior. These extra classes, called *Facades* (Gamma, Helm, Johnson, and Vlissides 1995), then delegate public operations to their shyer companions in the package.

Packages do not offer answers about how to reduce dependencies in your system, but they do help you to see what the dependencies are—and you can work to reduce dependencies only when you can see them. Package diagrams are a key tool for me in maintaining control over a system's overall structure.

Figure 7-2 is a more complex package diagram that contains additional constructs.

First, we see that I have added a Domain package that contains the orders and customers packages. This is useful because it means that I can draw dependencies to and from the overall package, instead of many separate dependencies.

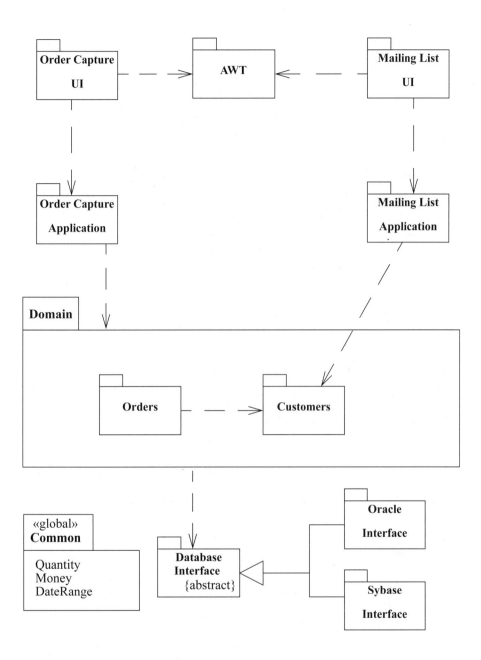

Figure 7-2: *Advanced Package Diagram*

When you show a package's contents, you put the name of the package in the "tab" and the contents inside the main box. These contents can be a list of classes, as in the Common package; another package diagram, as in Domain; or a class diagram (not shown, but the idea should be obvious by now).

Most of the time, I find it sufficient to list the key classes, but sometimes a further diagram is useful. In this case, I've shown that whereas the Order Capture application has a dependency to the entire Domain package, the Mailing List application is dependent only on the Customers package.

What does it mean to draw a dependency to a package that contains subpackages? In general, it means that the dependency summarizes a lower-level dependency. That is, there is some dependency to some element within the higher-level package, but you need a more detailed diagram to see the details. Again, the precise rules vary with the particular variety of dependency.

Figure 7-2 shows the Common package marked as «global». This means that all packages in the system have a dependency to Common. Obviously, you should use this construct sparingly, but common classes, such as Money, are used everywhere.

You can use generalization with packages. This means that the specific package must conform to the interface of the general package. This is comparable to the specification perspective of subtyping within class diagrams (see Chapter 4). Therefore, in accordance with Figure 7-2, the Database Broker can use either the Oracle Interface or the Sybase Interface. When generalization is used like this, the general package may be marked as {abstract} to show that it merely defines an interface that is implemented by a more specific package.

Generalization implies a dependency from the subtype to the supertype. (You don't need to show the extra dependency; the generalization itself is enough.) Putting abstract classes in a supertype package is a good way of breaking cycles in the dependency structure. In this situation, the database interface packages are responsible for loading and saving the domain objects in a database. They therefore need to know about the domain objects. However, the domain objects need to trigger the loading and saving.

The generalization allows us to put the necessary triggering interface— various load and save operations—into the database interface package. These operations are then implemented by classes within the subtype packages. There is then no dependency between the database interface package and the Oracle interface package, even though at run time, it will be the subtype package that gets called by the domain. But the domain thinks it is dealing only with the (simpler) database interface package. Polymorphism is just as useful for packages as it is with classes.

As a rule of thumb, it is a good idea to remove cycles in the dependency structure. I'm not convinced that you should remove all cycles, but you should certainly minimize them. If you do have them, try to contain them within a larger containing package. In practice, I have found cases in which I have not been able to avoid cycles between domain packages, but I do try to eliminate them from the interactions between the domain and external interfaces. Package generalization is a key element in doing this.

In an existing system, dependencies can be inferred by looking at the classes. This is a very useful task for a tool to perform. I find this handy if I am trying to improve the structure of an existing system. A useful early step is to divide the classes into packages and to analyze the dependences among the packages. Then I refactor to reduce the dependencies.

Collaborations

As well as containing classes, a package can contain collaborations. A **collaboration** is a name given to the interaction among two or more classes. Typically, this is an interaction, as described in an interaction diagram. Thus, the sequence diagram in Figure 7-3 describes the Make Sale collaboration.

This collaboration might show the implementation of an operation or the realization of a use case. You can model the collaboration before deciding what operation invokes it.

A collaboration can be described with more than one interaction diagram, with each one showing a different path. You can also add a class diagram to show the classes that participate in the collaboration. (See Figure 7-4.)

In addition to using collaborations within a package, you can use them to show common behavior across packages. If someone asks you about database interaction, you might need to point them to many packages and classes to see how that works, even though database interaction is only one aspect of these packages and classes. You can improve this by defining a database interaction collaboration. Within that collaboration, you show those aspects of the classes that are relevant, and interaction diagrams that show how they work.

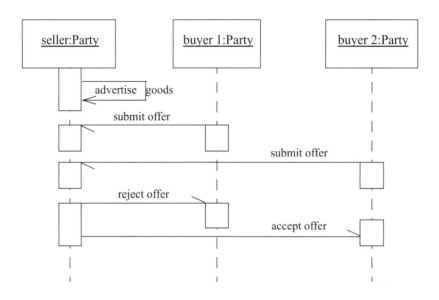

Figure 7-3: *Sequence Diagram for Making a Sale*

Often you may find that the same collaboration is used by different classes in the system. Each time, the basic way the classes work is the same, but classes and operations are named differently, and there may be minor differences in the implementation. You can illustrate this by parameterizing the collaboration.

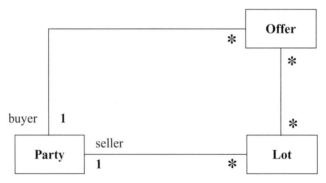

Figure 7-4: *Class Diagram for Make Sale Collaboration*

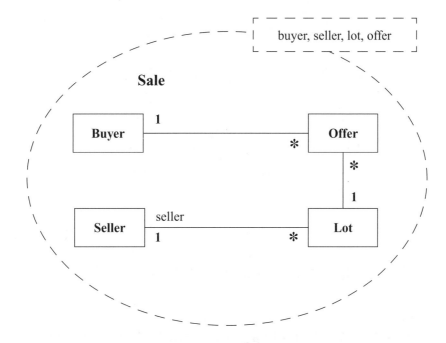

Figure 7-5: *Parameterized Collaboration for Sale*

First, you draw a diagram like Figure 7-5, which shows the various roles that various objects play in the collaboration. (Note that the classes in this diagram are not actual classes in the system; instead, they are roles in the collaboration.) You would then add interaction diagrams to show how these roles interact.

Next, you show how a set of classes participate in the collaboration, by drawing a diagram like Figure 7-6.

The UML also uses the term **pattern** as a synonym for parameterized collaboration. Calling it a pattern is controversial, as there is more to a pattern than this, but certainly this notation can be used to show where common patterns are used in a particular system.

You can also use this kind of notation in role-based modeling, within which you first model the collaborations and roles, and then come up with classes that implement these roles. You can find out more about this style of design in Reenskaug (1996).

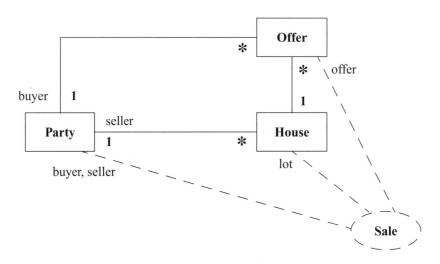

Figure 7-6: *Using the Sale Collaboration*

When to Use Package Diagrams and Collaborations

Packages are a vital tool for large projects. Use packages whenever a class diagram that encompasses the whole system is no longer legible on a single letter-size (or A4) sheet of paper.

Packages are particularly useful for testing. Although I do write some tests on a class-by-class basis, I prefer to do my unit testing on a package-by-package basis. Each package should have one or more test classes that test the behavior of the package.

I find collaborations useful whenever you want to refer to a particular interaction. Parameterized collaborations are useful when you have several similar collaborations in your system.

Where to Find Out More

The best discussion I know of packages is by Robert Martin (1995), whose book gives several examples of using Booch and C++, with a lot of attention paid to minimizing dependencies. You can also find valuable information in Wirfs-Brock (1990); the primary author refers to packages as subsystems.

Collaborations are a fairly new topic, so you'll find more discussion of them only in the more detailed UML books.

Chapter 8

State Diagrams

State diagrams are a familiar technique to describe the behavior of a system. They describe all of the possible states that a particular object can get into and how the object's state changes as a result of events that reach the object. In most OO techniques, state diagrams are drawn for a single class to show the lifetime behavior of a single object.

There are many forms of state diagrams, each with slightly different semantics. The UML style is based on David Harel's (1987) statechart.

Figure 8-1 shows a UML state diagram for an order in the order processing system I introduced earlier in the book. The diagram indicates the various states of an order.

We begin at the start point and show an initial transition into the Checking state. This transition is labeled "/get first item."

The syntax for a transition label has three parts, all of which are optional: *Event [Guard] / Action*. In this case, we have only the action "get first item." Once we perform that action, we enter the Checking state. This state has an activity associated with it, indicated by a label with the syntax *do/activity*. In this case, the activity is called "check item."

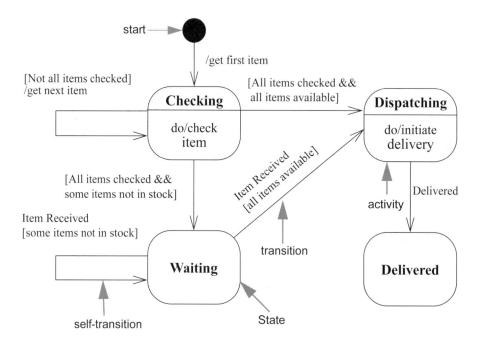

Figure 8-1: *State Diagram*

Note that I used the terms "action" for the transition and "activity" for the state. Although they are both processes, typically implemented by some method on Order, they are treated differently. **Actions** are associated with transitions and are considered to be processes that occur quickly and are not interruptible. **Activities** are associated with states and can take longer. An activity may be interrupted by some event.

Note that the definition of "quickly" depends on the kind of system you are producing. Within a hard real-time system, "quickly" may mean within a few machine instructions; for regular information systems, "quickly" might mean less than a few seconds.

When a transition has no event within its label, it means that the transition occurs as soon as any activity associated with the given state is completed. In this case, that means as soon as we are done with the Checking. Three transitions come out of the Checking state. All three have only guards on their label. A **guard** is a logical condition that will return only "true" or "false." A guarded transition occurs only if the guard resolves to "true."

Only one transition can be taken out of a given state, so we intend the guards to be mutually exclusive for any event. in Figure 8-1, we address three conditions.

1. If we have not checked all items, we get the next item and return to the Checking state to check it.

2. If we have checked all items and they were all in stock, we transition to the Dispatching state.

3. If we have checked all items but not all of them were in stock, we transition to the Waiting state.

I'll look at the Waiting state first. There are no activities for this state, so the given order sits in this state, waiting for an event. Both transitions out of the Waiting state are labeled with the Item Received event. This means that the order waits until it detects this event. At that point, it evaluates the guards on the transitions and makes the appropriate transition, either to Dispatching or back to Waiting.

Within the Dispatching state, we have an activity that initiates a delivery. There is also a single, unguarded transition triggered by the Delivered event. This indicates that the transition will always occur when that event occurs. Note, however, that the transition does *not* occur when the activity completes; instead, once the "initiate delivery" activity is finished, the given order remains in the Dispatching state until the Delivered event occurs.

The final thing to address is a transition named "cancelled." We want to be able to cancel an order at any point before it is delivered. We could do this by drawing separate transitions from each of the Checking, Waiting, and Dispatching states. A useful alternative is to create a **superstate** of all three states and then draw a single transition from that. The substates simply inherit any transitions on the superstate.

Figure 8-2 and Figure 8-3 show how these approaches reflect the same system behavior.

Even with only three duplicated transitions, Figure 8-2 looks rather cluttered. Figure 8-3 makes the whole picture much clearer, and if changes are needed later, it is harder to forget the cancelled event.

In the current examples, I have shown an activity within a state, indicated by text in the form *do/activity*. You can also indicate other things within a state.

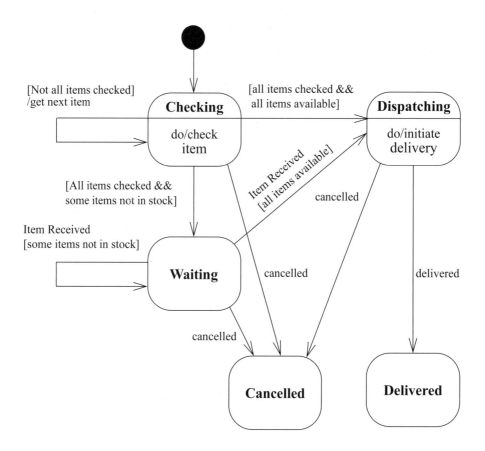

Figure 8-2: *State Diagram without Superstates*

If a state responds to an event with an action that does not cause a transition, you can show this by putting text in the form *eventName / actionName* in the state box.

There are a couple of other types of events in addition to named events from the outside.

- An event can be generated after a period of time. You indicate this with the keyword **after**. For instance, you might say *after (20 minutes)*.
- An event can be generated when a condition becomes true. You show this with the keyword **when**. For example, you could have *when(temperature > 100 degrees)*.

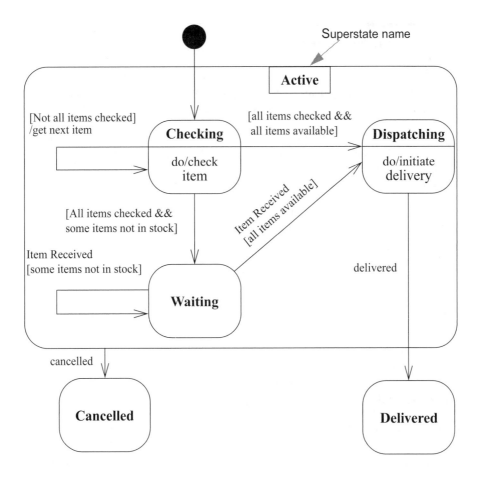

Figure 8-3: *State Diagram with Superstates*

There are also two special events, entry and exit. Any action that is marked as linked to the **entry** event is executed whenever the given state is entered via a transition. The action associated with the **exit** event is executed whenever the state is left via a transition. If you have a transition that goes back to the same state (this is called a **self-transition**) with an action, the exit action would be executed first, then the transition's action, and finally the entry action. If the state has an associated activity as well, that activity is executed after the entry action.

Concurrent State Diagrams

In addition to states of an order that are based on the availability of the items, there are also states that are based on payment authorization. If we look at these states, we might see a state diagram like the one in Figure 8-4.

Here we begin by doing an authorization. The "check payment" activity finishes by signaling that the payment is approved. If the payment is OK, the given order waits in the Authorized state until the "delivered" event occurs. Otherwise, the order enters the Rejected state.

The Order object exhibits a combination of the behaviors shown in Figure 8-1 and Figure 8-4. The associated states and the Cancelled state discussed earlier can be combined on a **concurrent state diagram** (see Figure 8-5).

Note that in Figure 8-5, I left out details of the internal states.

The concurrent sections of the state diagram are places in which at any point, the given order is in two different states, one from each diagram. When the order leaves the concurrent states, it is in only a single state. We can see that an order starts off in both the Checking and Authorizing states. If the "check payment" activity of the Authorizing state completes successfully first, the order will be in the Checking and Authorized states. If the "cancel" event occurs, the order will be in only the Cancelled state.

Concurrent state diagrams are useful when a given object has sets of independent behaviors. Note, however, that you should not get too many concurrent sets of behaviors occurring in a single object. If you have several complicated concurrent state diagrams for an object, you should consider splitting the object into separate objects.

When to Use State Diagrams

State diagrams are good at describing the behavior of an object across several use cases. State diagrams are not very good at describing behavior that involves a number of objects collaborating. As such, it is useful to combine state diagrams with other techniques.

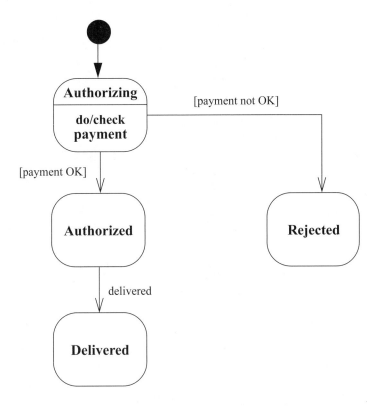

Figure 8-4: *Payment Authorization*

For instance, interaction diagrams (see Chapter 5) are good at describing the behavior of several objects in a single use case, and activity diagrams (see Chapter 9) are good at showing the general sequence of actions for several objects and use cases.

Not everyone finds state diagrams natural. Keep an eye on how people are working with them. It may be that your team does not find state diagrams useful to its way of working. That is not a big problem; as always, you should remember to use the mix of techniques that works for you.

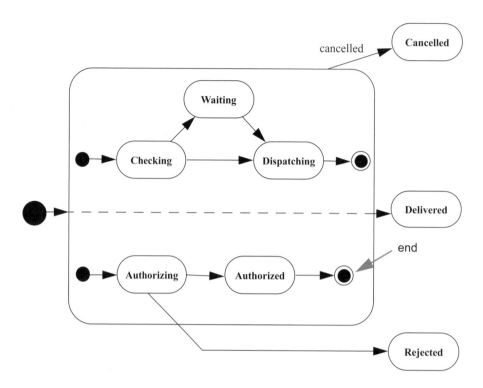

Figure 8-5: *Concurrent State Diagram*

If you do use state diagrams, don't try to draw them for every class in the system. Although this approach is often used by high-ceremony completists, it is almost always a waste of effort. Use state diagrams only for those classes that exhibit interesting behavior, where building the state diagram helps you understand what is going on. Many people find that UI and control objects have the kind of behavior that is useful to depict with a state diagram.

Where to Find Out More

Both the *User Guide* (Booch, Rumbaugh, and Jacobson 1999) and the *Reference Manual* (Rumbaugh, Jacobson, and Booch 1999) have more information on state diagrams. Real-time designers tend to use state models a lot, so it's no surprise that Douglass (1998) has a lot to say about state diagrams, including information on how to implement them.

If you use state diagrams heavily, you should read the discussion in Cook and Daniels (1994). Although there are differences in semantics between statecharts at that time and those in the UML, the authors do go into detailed issues that you should be aware of if you are using state diagrams.

Chapter 9

Activity Diagrams

Activity diagrams are one of most unexpected parts of the UML.

Unlike most other techniques in the UML, the activity diagram doesn't have clear origins in the previous works of the three amigos. Rather, the **activity diagram** combines ideas from several techniques: the event diagrams of Jim Odell, SDL state modeling techniques, workflow modeling, and Petri nets. These diagrams are particularly useful in connection with workflow and in describing behavior that has a lot of parallel processing.

I'm going to describe activity diagrams in more detail than they really warrant in this short book. The reason is that they are one of the least understood areas of the UML, and current UML books are particularly lacking in discussing them.

In Figure 9-1, the core symbol is the **activity state**, or simply **activity**. An activity is a state of doing something: either a real-world process, such as typing a letter, or the execution of a software routine, such as a method on a class.

The activity diagram describes the sequencing of activities, with support for both conditional and parallel behavior. An activity diagram is a variant of a state diagram in which most, if not all, the states are activity states. Thus, much of the terminology follows that of state diagrams.

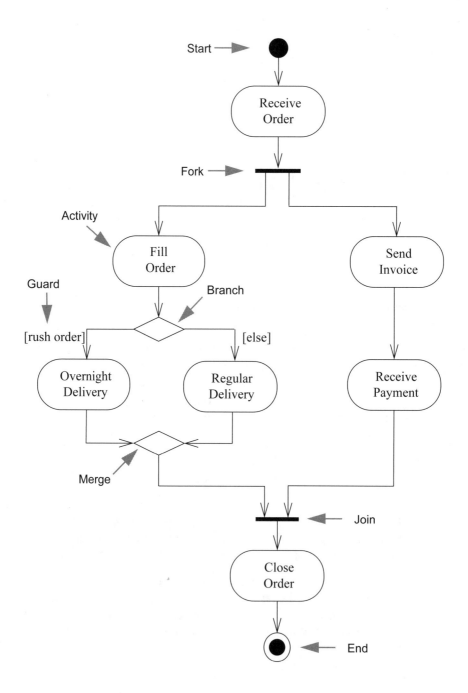

Figure 9-1: *Activity Diagram*

Conditional behavior is delineated by branches and merges.

A **branch** has a single incoming transition and several guarded outgoing transitions. Only one of the outgoing transitions can be taken, so the guards should be mutually exclusive. Using [else] as a guard indicates that the "else" transition should be used if all the other guards on the branch are false.

In Figure 9-1, after an order is filled, there is a branch. If you have a rush order, you do an overnight delivery; otherwise, you do a regular delivery.

A **merge** has multiple input transitions and a single output. A merge marks the end of conditional behavior started by a branch.

You don't have to show the explicit diamond for branches and merges. An activity state, like any state, can have multiple guarded output transitions and multiple input transitions. Use diamonds if you want to make the branches and merges clear in the diagram.

Parallel behavior is indicated by forks and joins.

A **fork** has one incoming transition and several outgoing transitions. When the incoming transition is triggered, all of the outgoing transitions are taken in parallel. Thus, in Figure 9-1, after you receive an order, you fill the order and send the invoice in parallel.

The diagram says that these activities can occur in parallel. Essentially, this means that the sequence between them is irrelevant. I could fill the order, send the invoice, deliver, and then receive payment; or, I could send the invoice, receive the payment, then fill the order and deliver—you get the picture.

I can also do these activities by interleaving. I grab the first line item from stores, type up the invoice, grab the second line item, put the invoice in an envelope, and so forth. Or, I could do some of this simultaneously: type up the invoice with one hand while I reach into my stores with another. Any of these is correct, according to the diagram.

The activity diagram allows me to choose the order in which to do things. In other words, it merely states the essential sequencing rules I have to follow. This is the key difference between an activity diagram and a flowchart: flowcharts are normally limited to sequential processes, whereas activity diagrams can handle parallel processes.

This is important for business modeling. Businesses often have unnecessarily sequential processes. A technique like this that encourages parallel behavior is valuable in these situations because it encourages people to move away from unnecessary sequences in their behavior and to spot opportunities to do things in parallel. This can improve the efficiency and responsiveness of business processes.

Activity diagrams are also useful for concurrent programs, since you can graphically lay out what threads you have and when they need to synchronize.

When you get parallel behavior, you need to synchronize. We don't close the order until it is delivered and paid for. We show this with the **join** before the Close Order activity. With a join, the outgoing transition is taken only when all the states on the incoming transitions have completed their activities.

Forks and joins must match. In the simplest case, this means that every time you have a fork, you must have a join that joins together the threads started by that fork. (This rule comes from the fact that the activity diagram is presently a form of state diagram.)

However, there are several extensions to this rule.

- A thread that comes out of a fork can itself fork, with the new threads coming back together before reaching the matching join.

- If a thread coming out of a fork goes straight into another fork, you can remove the second fork and just have the threads from the second fork coming out of the first fork. Thus, in Figure 9-2, I have removed a fork between the food preparation activities and the opening fork. Similarly, if a join goes right into another join, you can eliminate the first join and have the threads go right into the second join. This is a notational short-hand to remove clutter from the diagram; it has the same semantic meaning as if the extra forks and joins were there.

- An advanced construct called the **synch state** allows you to synchronize in places where the matching forks and joins rule would otherwise prevent you from doing so. For details about this construct, see the *Reference Manual* (Rumbaugh, Jacobson, and Booch 1999) or the standard.

There is an exception to the rule that all incoming states on a join must have finished before the join can be taken. You can add a condition to a thread coming out of a fork. The result is a **conditional thread**. During execution, if the condition on a conditional thread is false, that thread is considered to be complete as far as the join is concerned. So in Figure 9-2, even if I don't feel like wine, I would still be able to eat my Spaghetti Carbonara. (I must confess, though, that I've never had to test this rule when executing this diagram!)

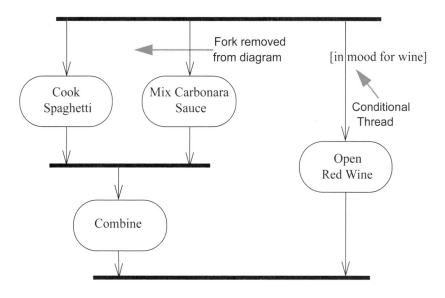

Figure 9-2: *Forks, Joins, and Conditional Threads*

Decomposing an Activity

An activity can be broken down into subactivities. This works much the same as a superstate and substates do on a state diagram. You can just show the superstate on the parent diagram, or you can show the superstate and its internal behavior inside it, as I have in Figure 9-3. In this case, I've given the delivery activity both a start and an end. You can also draw transitions directly into, or out of, the subsidiary diagram. The advantages of the explicit start and end states are that the delivery activity can be used in other contexts, and the parent diagram is decoupled from the contents of the subsidiary diagram.

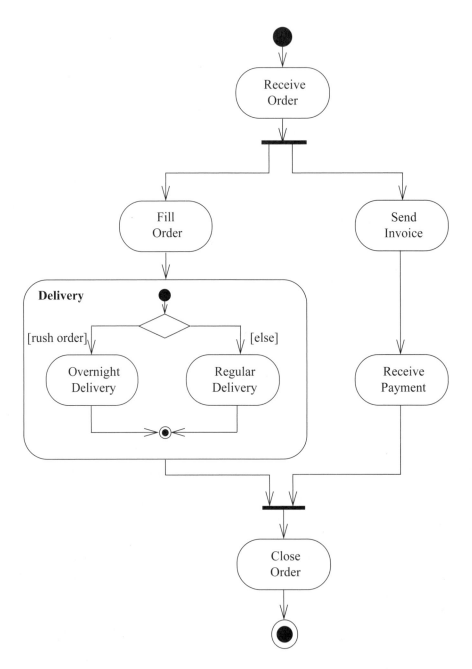

Figure 9-3: *Using a Composite Activity for Delivery*

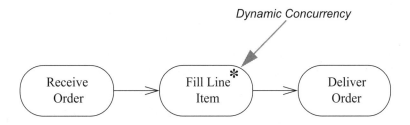

Figure 9-4: *Dynamic Concurrency*

Dynamic Concurrency

Dynamic concurrency allows you to show iterations without having to construct a loop.

In Figure 9-4, the activity Fill Line Item is executed once for each line item on the order. The multiplicity marker (*) indicates that the activity is executed many times. The transition to Deliver Order is triggered only when all the line items have been filled. If several activities need to be executed together in some manner, you can show this by making Fill Line Item a composite activity.

Swimlanes

Activity diagrams tell you what happens, but they do not tell you who does what. In programming, this means that the diagram does not convey which class is responsible for each activity.

In domain modeling, this means that the diagram does not convey which people or departments are responsible for each activity. One way around this is to label each activity with the responsible class or human. This works, but does not offer the same clarity as interaction diagrams (see Chapter 5) for showing communication among objects.

Swimlanes are a way around this.

To use swimlanes, you must arrange your activity diagrams into vertical zones separated by lines. Each zone represents the responsibilities of a particular class or, in the case of Figure 9-5, a particular department.

Swimlanes are good in that they combine the activity diagram's depiction of logic with the interaction diagram's depiction of responsibility. However, they can be difficult to draw on a complex diagram. I have used nonlinear zones on occasion, which is better than nothing. (Sometimes you have to stop trying to say too much in one diagram.)

When they draw an activity diagram, some people make sure to assign activities to objects. Other people are happy to work with the activity diagram first, to get an overall sense of the behavior, and assign the activities to objects later. I've seen people who assign immediately get emotional about those who defer assignment; they make unpleasant accusations of drawing dataflow diagrams and not being object-oriented.

I confess that I often draw an activity diagram without assigning behavior to objects until later. I find it useful to figure out one thing at a time. This is particularly true when I'm doing business modeling and encouraging a domain expert to think of new ways of doing things. That way works for me. Others prefer to assign behavior to objects immediately. You should do whatever you're more comfortable doing. The important thing is to assign activities to classes before you are done. For that, I prefer to use an interaction diagram (see Chapter 5).

When to Use Activity Diagrams

Like most behavioral modeling techniques, activity diagrams have definite strengths and weaknesses, so they are best used in combination with other techniques.

The great strength of activity diagrams lies in the fact that they support and encourage parallel behavior. This makes them a great tool for workflow modeling and, in principle, for multithreaded programming. Their great disadvantage is that they do not make the links among actions and objects very clear.

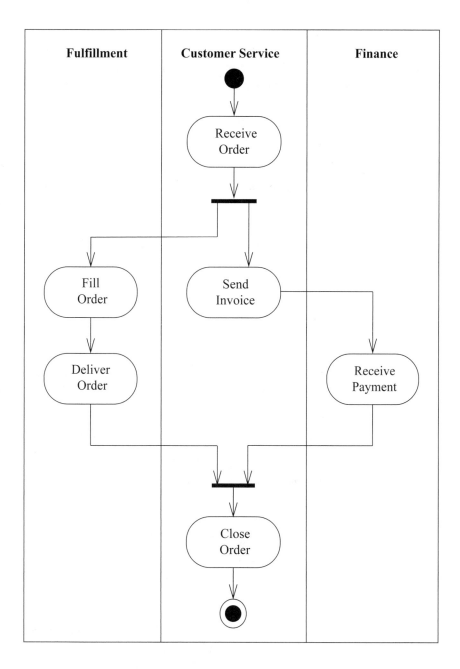

Figure 9-5: *Swimlanes*

You can define a link to an object by labeling an activity with an object name or by using swimlanes, which divide an activity diagram based on responsibilities, but this does not have the simple immediacy of interaction diagrams (see Chapter 5). For this reason, some people feel that using activity diagrams is not object-oriented and, thus, bad. I've found that the technique can be very useful, and I don't throw useful tools out of my toolkit.

I like to use activity diagrams in the following situations:

- *Analyzing a use case.* At this stage, I'm not interested in allocating actions to objects; I just need to understand what actions need to take place and what the behavioral dependencies are. I allocate methods to objects later and show those allocations with an interaction diagram.

- *Understanding workflow.* Even before I get into use cases, I find activity diagrams very useful for understanding a business process. I can easily draw these diagrams together with business experts to understand how a business operates and how it may change.

- *Describing a complicated sequential algorithm.* In this case, an activity diagram is really nothing more than a UML-compliant flowchart. The usual pros and cons of flowcharts apply.

- *Dealing with multithreaded applications.* I have not personally used activity diagrams for this purpose, but I have heard some good reports.

Don't use activity diagrams in the following situations:

- *Trying to see how objects collaborate.* An interaction diagram is simpler and gives you a clearer picture of collaborations.

- *Trying to see how an object behaves over its lifetime.* Use a state diagram (see Chapter 8) for that.

- *Representing complex conditional logic.* Use a truth table.

The work on UML 1.3 added a lot more rigor and precision to activity diagrams. However, that's a mixed blessing. The problem is that when you use these diagrams for conceptual modeling, much of this rigor gets in the way. In these situations, you aren't aiming for complete accuracy, just a general overview of how things work. In any case, you're unlikely to get it right, even if you try, unless you're able to execute and test the diagram. Remember Bertrand Meyer's phrase: "Bubbles don't crash."

On the other hand, by having a standard for state and activity diagrams, there's a more stable foundation for tool developers to build tools that will execute these diagrams. Such tools will allow you to run and test these diagrams.

Where to Find Out More

Little information exists on activity diagrams. The *Reference Manual* (Rumbaugh, Jacobson, and Booch 1999) provides a lot of details, but doesn't provide a tutorial on how they work. The *User Guide* (Booch, Jacobson, and Rumbaugh 1999) doesn't get into enough detail to answer the kinds of questions you'll run into when you try to use the technique in anger. Ideally, somebody will fill this gap in the not too distant future.

Chapter 10

Physical Diagrams

The UML provides two kinds of physical diagrams: deployment diagrams and component diagrams.

Deployment Diagrams

A **deployment diagram** shows the physical relationships among software and hardware components in the delivered system. A deployment diagram is a good place to show how components and objects are routed and move around a distributed system.

Each **node** on a deployment diagram represents some kind of computational unit—in most cases, a piece of hardware. The hardware may be a simple device or sensor, or it could be a mainframe.

Figure 10-1 shows a PC connected to a UNIX server through TCP/IP. **Connections** among nodes show the communication paths over which the system will interact.

Component Diagrams

A **component diagram** shows the various components in a system and their dependencies.

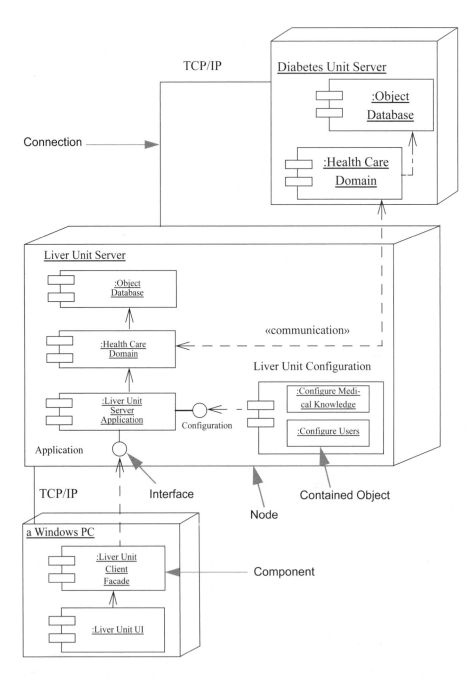

Figure 10-1: *Deployment Diagram*

A **component** represents a physical module of code. A component is often the same as a package, but it may be different, since components represent the physical packaging of code. As such, a single class may be present in multiple components, but that class can be defined in only one package. For example, the Java *string* class is part of the java.lang package, but it turns up in lots of components.

The **dependencies** among the components show how changes to one component may cause other components to change. There is quite a range of dependencies that you can use, including communication and compilation dependencies. I often use these kinds of dependencies to show which components communicate with one another.

Combining Component and Deployment Diagrams

Although you can draw separate component and deployment diagrams, you can also place the component diagram on the deployment diagram, as I have done with Figure 10-1. You can do this to show which components run on which nodes.

So in the diagram, the Liver Unit UI and the Liver Unit Client Facade both run on a Windows PC. The Liver Unit UI is dependent on the Liver Unit Client Facade, since it calls specific methods on the facade. Although the communication is two-way, in the sense that the Facade returns data, the Facade is not aware of who is calling it and is thus not dependent on the UI. In contrast, in the communication between the two Health Care Domain components, both are aware that they are talking to another Health Care Domain component, so the communication dependency is two-way. The two domain components run on separate nodes.

A component may have more than one interface, in which case you can see which components communicate with each interface. On Figure 10-1, the server application has two interfaces. One interface is used by the application facade running on a PC; the other interface is used by a configuration component running on the server.

The use of multiple Health Care Domain components is hidden from its clients. Each Health Care Domain component has a local database.

People often draw these kinds of diagrams with symbols that look like the various elements. For instance, they use special icons for servers, PCs, and databases. This is legal in the UML: You can treat each icon as a stereotype of the appropriate diagram element. Usually, such icons make the diagram easier to understand, although they get messy if you show nodes and components together, as I do on Figure 10-1.

When to Use Physical Diagrams

Most people draw this kind of information informally, but gradually people are formalizing the diagrams to fit in with the UML. I draw these diagrams whenever I have to show physical information that is different from the associated logical information. Most times, I find that I draw at least one diagram that shows nodes and major components in the style of Figure 10-1. I use pictorial icons if I can do so without the diagram getting too cluttered.

Chapter 11

UML and Programming

So far, I have discussed a lot of notation. One large question looms: How does a programmer actually *use* the UML as part of the daily grind of programming? I'll answer this by talking about how I use the UML when I'm programming, even on a small scale. I won't go into a lot of detail, but I hope this will give you a sense of what you can do with the UML.

Let's imagine a computer system designed to pull together information about patients for a hospital.

Various health care professionals make observations about patients. This simple system will allow someone to get information about those observations and to add additional observations. As this is a short book, I will wave my arms about the database links and the UI and consider only the basic domain classes.

This is such a simple example that it has but a single use case, named "review and add patient observations." We can elaborate on that with a few scenarios.

- Ask for the latest heart rate of a patient.
- Ask for the blood type of a patient.

- Update a patient's level of consciousness.
- Update a patient's heart rate. The system marks the rate as slow, normal, or fast, according to the system's built-in ranges.

My first step in the process is to come up with a conceptual model that describes the concepts in this domain. At this stage, I'm not thinking about how the software is going to work, only about how to organize concepts in the minds of the doctors and nurses. I'll start with a model based on several analysis patterns from Fowler (1997): *Observation*, *Quantity*, *Range*, and *Phenomenon with Range*.

Patient Observation: Domain Model

Figure 11-1 shows the initial domain model for our system.

How do these concepts represent the information in the domain?

I'll start with the simple concepts of Quantity, Unit, and Range. Quantity represents a dimensioned value, such as 6 feet—a quantity with amount of 6 and unit of feet. Units are simply those categories of measurement with which we want to deal. Range allows us to talk about ranges as a single concept—for instance, a range of 4 feet to 6 feet is represented as a single Range object with an upper bound of 6 feet and a lower bound of 4 feet. In general, ranges can be expressed in terms of anything that can be compared (using the operators <, >, <=, >=, and =), so the upper and lower bounds of a Range are both magnitudes. (Quantities are a kind of magnitude.)

Each observation made by a doctor or a nurse is an instance of the Observation concept and is either a Measurement or a Category Observation. So a measurement of a height of 6 feet for Martin Fowler would be represented as an instance of Measurement. Associated with this Measurement are the amount 6 feet, the Phenomenon Type "height," and the Patient named Martin Fowler. Phenomenon Types represent the things that can be measured: height, weight, heart rate, and so forth.

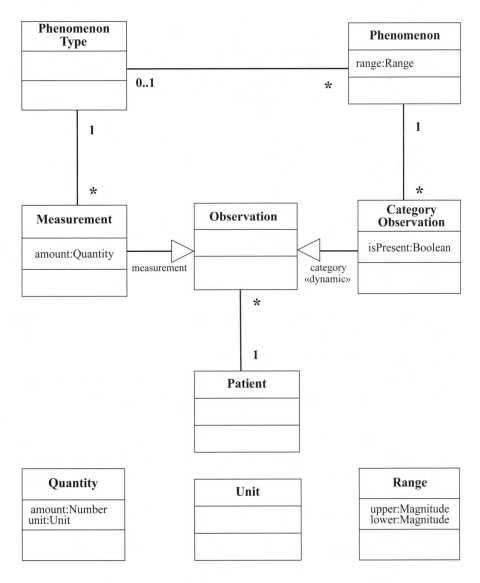

Figure 11-1: *Patient Observation Domain Model*

An observation that Martin Fowler's blood type is O would be represented as a Category Observation whose associated Phenomenon is "blood group O." This Phenomenon is linked to the Phenomenon Type "blood group."

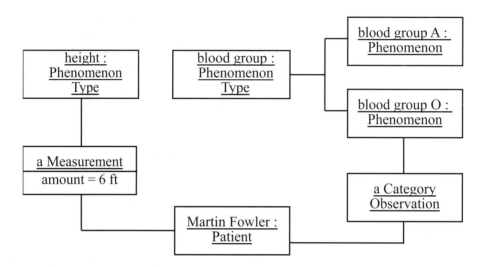

Figure 11-2: *Patient Observation Object Diagram*

The object diagram in Figure 11-2 should make things a little clearer at this point.

Figure 11-3 shows that we can make an Observation serve as both a Measurement and a Category Observation by stating that a Measurement of "90 beats per minute" can also be a Category Observation whose associated Phenomenon is "fast heart rate."

At this stage, I have looked at only the representation of the concepts; I haven't thought much about behavior. I don't always do that, but it seems an appropriate starting point for a problem that is mainly about dealing with information.

For the moment, I'm still talking about patient observation *concepts*, just as I would be doing with a doctor or a nurse. (Indeed, that is what happened in real life. The conceptual models were built by a couple of doctors and a nurse, with me helping.) To make the move to an object-oriented program, I have to decide how to deal with the conceptual picture in terms of software. For this exercise, I have chosen the Java programming language. (I had to get Java into this book somehow!)

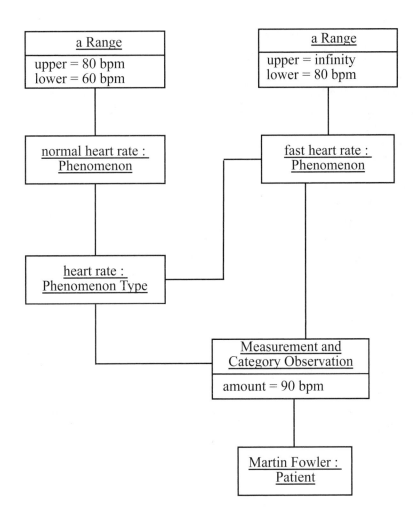

Figure 11-3: *Another Patient Observation Object Diagram*

Most of these concepts will work well as Java classes. Patient, Phenomenon Type, Phenomenon, Unit, and Quantity will work with no trouble. The two sticky items are Range and Observation.

Range is an issue because I want to form a range of quantities for a Phenomenon. I could do this by creating a "magnitude" interface and stating that Quantity implements that interface, but that would leave me with a lot of downcasting. This does not happen in Smalltalk, and I can use parameterized types in C++. For this exercise, I prefer to use a QuantityRange class that uses the *Range* pattern.

My problem with Observation is that an Observation can be both a Category Observation and a Measurement at the same time (see Figure 11-3). In Java, like most other programming languages, we have only single classification. I decided to deal with this by allowing any Observation to have an associated Phenomenon, which effectively lets the Observation class implement both the Observation and Category Observation concepts.

These decisions do not result in a perfect state of affairs, but they are the kind of pragmatic imperfection that allows work to get done. Don't try to do software that exactly maps the conceptual perspective. Try, instead, to be faithful to the spirit of conceptual perspective but still realistic considering the tools you are using.

Patient Observation: Specification Model

Figure 11-4 reflects modifications I made to the domain model to take into account some of the factors associated with a target language.

The patient observation model is now at the specification perspective. It shows the class interfaces rather than the classes themselves. I might keep the conceptual model for another day, but more likely, I will work only with the specification model from this point forward. I try not to keep too many models around. My rule of thumb is that if I cannot keep a model up to date, it goes in the bin. (I know I'm lazy, too!)

Now let's look at the *behavior* associated with our patient observation model.

The first scenario asks for the latest heart rate of the patient. The first question is: Whose responsibility is it to handle this request? The Patient seems the natural choice. The Patient needs to look at all its observations, determine which are measurements of the Phenomenon Type "heart rate," and find the latest value. To do this, I will have to add a timepoint to Measurement. Because this can apply to other observations as well, I'll add it to Observation, too.

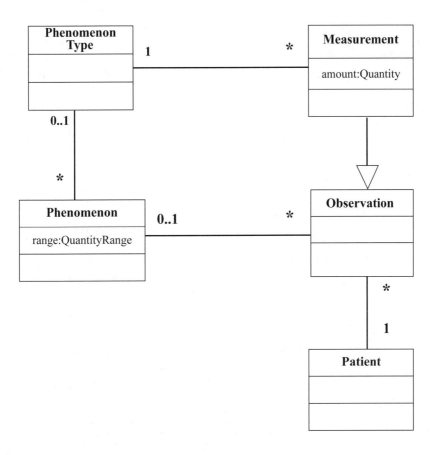

Figure 11-4: *Patient Observation Specification Model*

Patient has a similar responsibility for returning a Phenomenon: Find the latest Category Observation that has a Phenomenon for the given Phenomenon Type.

Figure 11-5 shows operations that I've added to Patient to reflect my thinking.

Don't try too hard to come up with operations if they are not obvious just yet. The most important thing to go for is a statement of responsibility. If you can cast that in the form of an operation, that's fine; otherwise, a short phrase is useful in describing the responsibility.

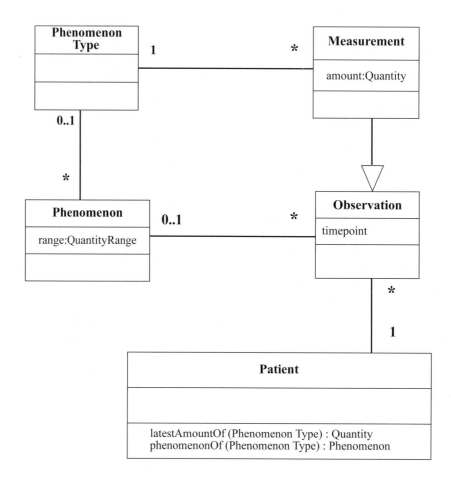

Figure 11-5: *Patient Observation Operations*

Updating the patient's level of consciousness involves creating a new Observation of the appropriate Phenomenon. In doing that, the user would usually like to pick a Phenomenon from a pop-up list. We can handle that by getting the Phenomenon objects associated with a particular Phenomenon Type, as this responsibility is implied by the association between the two.

In adding a measurement, we need to create a new Measurement. An additional complication comes from the fact that the Measurement needs to look to see whether there is a Phenomenon that can be assigned. Here the Measurement can ask its associated Phenomenon Type whether there is a Phenomenon to assign.

There is some collaboration among the objects here. This suggests that this is a good place for a sequence diagram (see Figure 11-6).

Do you *have* to draw all of these diagrams?

Not necessarily. Much depends on how well you can visualize what is going on and how easy it is to work in your programming language. In Smalltalk, it's often just as easy to write the code as it is to think with the diagrams. With C++, the diagrams are more useful.

The diagrams don't have to be works of art. I usually sketch them out on a paper pad or a small whiteboard. I transfer them to a drawing tool (or CASE tool) only if I think it's worth the effort of keeping them up to date because they help clarify the behavior of the classes. At this point in a project, I might also use CRC cards (see page 75) in addition to or instead of the diagrams I've been describing in this chapter.

Moving to Code

Now we can take a look at some of the code that implements the ideas I discussed in the previous sections. I'll begin with Phenomenon Type and Phenomenon, since they are quite closely linked.

The first thing to think about is the association between them: Should the interface allow navigability in both directions? In this case, I think so because both directions will be valuable and they are closely linked concepts, in any case. Indeed, I am happy to implement the association with pointers in both directions, too. I shall make it an immutable association, however, as these are objects that are set up and then left alone—they are not modified often, and when they are, we can create them again.

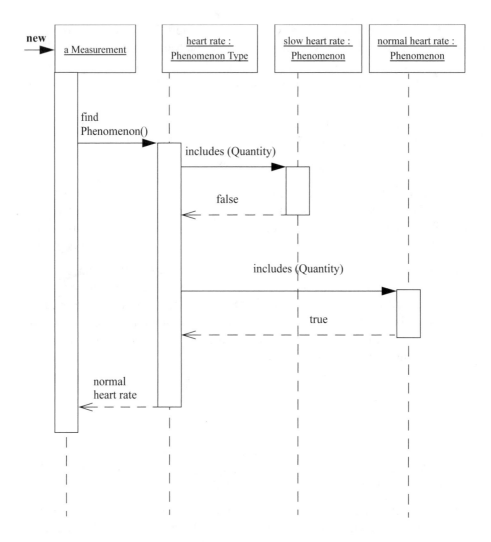

Figure 11-6: *Patient Observation Sequence Diagram*

Some people have trouble with two-way links. I don't find them troublesome if I ensure that one class takes the overall responsibility for keeping the link up to date, assisted by a "friend" or helper method, as necessary.

Let's look at some declarations.

```
public class PhenomenonType extends DomainObject {
 public PhenomenonType(String name) {
  super(name);
 };

 void friendPhenomenonAdd(Phenomenon newPhenomenon) {
  // RESTRICTED: only used by Phenomenon
  _phenomena.addElement(newPhenomenon);
 };

 public void setPhenomena(String[] names) {
  for (int i = 0; i < names.length; i++)
   new Phenomenon(names[i], this);
 };

 public Enumeration phenomena() {
  return _phenomena.elements();
 };

 private Vector _phenomena = new Vector();

 private QuantityRange _validRange;
}
```

I use the convention of adding an underscore before all fields. It helps me avoid getting my names confused.

```
public class Phenomenon extends DomainObject {
 public Phenomenon(String name, PhenomenonType type) {
  super (name);
  _type = type;
  _type.friendPhenomenonAdd(this);
 };
 public PhenomenonType phenomenonType() {
  return _type;
 };

 private PhenomenonType _type;
```

```
    private QuantityRange _range;
}


package observations;

public class DomainObject {
  public DomainObject(String name) {
    _name = name;
  };

  public DomainObject()      {};

  public String name() {
   return _name;
  };

  public String toString() {
   return _name;
  };

  protected String _name = "no name";
}
```

I've added a DomainObject class, which knows about names and will do any other behavior that I want all of my domain classes to do.

I can now set up these objects with code along the lines of the following:

```
PhenomenonType sex =
  new PhenomenonType("gender").persist();
String[] sexes = {"male", "female"};
sex.setPhenomena(sexes);
```

The **persist()** operation stores the Phenomenon Type in a registry object so that you can get it again later with a static **get()** method. I'll skip the details of that.

Next, I'll put in the code to add observations to a patient. Here I don't want all the associations to be two-way. I have the patient hang on to a collection of observations, since they are used in the context of a patient.

```
public class Observation extends DomainObject {
 public Observation(Phenomenon relevantPhenomenon,
   Patient patient, Date whenObserved) {
    _phenomenon = relevantPhenomenon;
    patient.observationsAdd(this);
    _whenObserved = whenObserved;
 };

 private Phenomenon _phenomenon;

 private Date _whenObserved;
}


public class Patient extends DomainObject {
 public Patient(String name) {
   super(name);
 };

 void observationsAdd(Observation newObs) {
   _observations.addElement(newObs);
 };

 private Vector _observations = new Vector();
}
```

With this I can create observations.

```
new Patient("Adams").persist();
new Observation(PhenomenonType.get("gender").
 phenomenonNamed("male"), Patient.get("Adams"),
 new Date (96, 3, 1) );
```

```
class PhenomenonType {
 public Phenomenon phenomenonNamed(String name) {
  Enumeration e = phenomena();
  while (e.hasMoreElements() )
  {
   Phenomenon each = (Phenomenon)e.nextElement();
   if (each.name().equals(name))
    return each;
  };

  return null;
 }
```

After creating observations, I need to be able to find the latest phenomenon.

```
class Patient
 public Phenomenon phenomenonOf
  (PhenomenonType phenomenonType)
 {
  return (latestObservation(phenomenonType) ==
   null ? new NullPhenomenon() :
   latestObservation(phenomenonType).phenomenon() );
 }

 private Observation
  latestObservation(PhenomenonType value) {
  return latestObservationIn(observationsOf(value) );
 }

 private Enumeration
  observationsOf(PhenomenonType value) {
   Vector result = new Vector();
   Enumeration e = observations();
   while (e.hasMoreElements() )
   {
    Observation each = (Observation) e.nextElement();
    if (each.phenomenonType() == value)
     result.addElement(each);
   };
   return result.elements();
 }
```

```
private Observation latestObservationIn
  (Enumeration observationEnum) {
  if (!observationEnum.hasMoreElements() )
   return null;
  Observation result =
   (Observation)observationEnum.nextElement();
  if (!observationEnum.hasMoreElements() )
   return result;

  do
  {
   Observation each =
    (Observation)observationEnum.nextElement();
   if (each.whenObserved().
    after(result.whenObserved() ) )
     result = each;
  }

  while (observationEnum.hasMoreElements() );

  return result;
 }

class Observation
 public PhenomenonType phenomenonType() {
  return _phenomenon.phenomenonType();
 }
```

Several methods combine to do this. You could draw a diagram to show this, but I tend not to bother. The way I decompose a method has more to do with refactoring (see page 29) than it does with prior design.

We can now look at adding the behavior for measurements.

First, let's see the definition of the Measurement class and its constructor.

```
public class Measurement extends Observation {
 public Measurement(Quantity amount,
  PhenomenonType phenomenonType,
  Patient patient, Date whenObserved) {
   initialize (patient, whenObserved);
```

```
  _amount = amount;
  _phenomenonType = phenomenonType;
 };

 public PhenomenonType phenomenonType() {
  return _phenomenonType;
 };

 public String toString() {
  return _phenomenonType + ": " + _amount;
 };

 private Quantity _amount;

 private PhenomenonType _phenomenonType;
}


class Observation
 protected void initialize(Patient patient,
  Date whenObserved) {
   patient.observationsAdd(this);
   _whenObserved = whenObserved;
 }
```

Note that a class diagram gives us a good start on developing this.

We again need the latest measurement.

```
Class Patient
 public Quantity latestAmountOf(PhenomenonType value) {
  return ((latestMeasurement(value) == null) ) ?
  new NullQuantity():latestMeasurement(value).amount();
 }

 private Measurement
  latestMeasurement(PhenomenonType value) {
   if (latestObservation(value) == null)
    return null;
   if (!latestObservation(value).isMeasurement() )
    return null;
   return (Measurement)latestObservation(value);
 }
```

In both of these cases, the class diagram suggests basic structure, and we add behavior to it to support more interesting queries.

At this stage, we could describe our position with the specification-perspective class diagram shown in Figure 11-7.

Take a look at how this diagram stresses interface over implementation. I've modeled the role from Phenomenon Type to Phenomenon as a qualified role because that's the primary interface on Phenomenon Type. Similarly, I've shown Observation with a link to Phenomenon Type because the interface exists there, even though the measurement is the only one with a direct pointer to Phenomenon.

Looking at this diagram, we can see that the only difference between Measurement and Observation is that Measurement has a quantity. We could remove the Measurement class entirely from the specification model by allowing any observation to have a (potentially null) quantity.

We could still have a separate Measurement class, which would have *amount* and *phenomenon type* fields, but nobody outside the package would be aware of the class's existence. We would need to add Factory methods (Gamma, Helm, Johnson, and Vlissides 1995) either on Observation or on Patient to allow the appropriate class to be created.

I will leave that change as an exercise for the reader and move on to assigning a Phenomenon automatically for a Measurement.

Figure 11-7 illustrates the general process.

First, we need to add a method call to Measurement's constructor.

```
Class Measurement
  public Measurement (Quantity amount,
  PhenomenonType phenomenonType,
  Patient patient, Date whenObserved)
    initialize (patient, whenObserved);
    _amount = amount;
    _phenomenonType = phenomenonType;
    _phenomenon =  calculatePhenomenonFor (_amount);
```

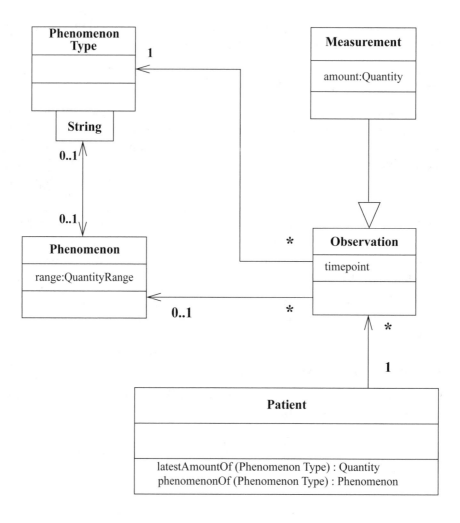

Figure 11-7: *Another Patient Observation Specification Model*

This delegates the task to Phenomenon Type.

```
Class Measurement
 public Phenomenon calculatePhenomenonFor(Quantity arg)
 {
  return _phenomenonType.phenomenonIncluding(arg);
 }
```

This asks each phenomenon in turn.

```
Class PhenomenonType
  public Phenomenon phenomenonIncluding (Quantity arg) {
    Enumeration e = phenomena();
    while (e.hasMoreElements())
    {
     Phenomenon each = (Phenomenon) e.nextElement();
     if (each.includes(arg))
      return each;
    };

    return null;
  }
Class Phenomenon
  public boolean includes (Quantity arg) {
    return (_range == null ? false:_range.includes(arg));
  }
```

The code flows out well from the sequence diagram. In practice, I usually use a sequence diagram to rough out the interaction and then make some changes as I code it. If the interaction is important, I will update the sequence chart as part of my documentation. If I think that the sequence chart will not add much clarity to the code, I file the rough sequence chart in the circular filing cabinet.

This is a brief example of how to use the UML with a programming language, but it should give you a good idea of the process. You don't have to be on a high-ceremony project to find using bits of the UML handy. You don't have to use all of it, just the bits you find useful.

Sketching out a design with a class diagram and an interaction diagram can help get your thoughts in order and make it easier to code. I think of these sketches as fast prototypes. You don't have to hold on to the diagrams later, but you may find it easier for yourself and others to understand the code if you do.

You don't need a fancy and expensive CASE tool. A whiteboard and a simple drawing tool on your computer will do fine. Of course, there are useful CASE tools, and if you are involved in a larger project, you might consider getting one.

If you do, compare it to the baseline of a simple drawing tool and a word processor. (It's amazing how much you can do with Visio and Word, for instance.) If the tool has code generation, look carefully at how it generates code. Code generation forces the CASE tool to take a very particular interpretation of the diagrams, which will affect the way you draw the diagrams and what the diagrams mean.

You can find more about this example via my Web site. The version of the example at the site goes more deeply into some of the layering issues involved in getting this model to a user interface.

Appendix A

Techniques and Their Uses

Technique	Purpose
Activity Diagram	Shows behavior with control structure. Can show many objects over many uses, many objects in single use case, or implementation of method. Encourages parallel behavior.
Class Diagram	Shows static structure of concepts, types, and classes. Concepts show how users think about the world; types show interfaces of software components; classes show implementation of software components.
CRC Cards	Helps get to essence of class's purpose. Good for exploring how to implement use case. Use if getting bogged down with details or if learning object approach to design.
Deployment Diagram	Shows physical layout of components on hardware nodes.

Technique	*Purpose*
Design by Contract	Provides rigorous definition of operation's purpose and class's legal state. Encode these in class to enhance debugging.
Interaction Diagram	Shows how several objects collaborate in single use case.
Package Diagram	Shows groups of classes and dependencies among them.
Patterns	Offers useful bits of analysis, design, and coding techniques. Good examples to learn from; starting point for designs.
Refactoring	Helps in making changes to working program to improve structure. Use when code is getting in the way of good design.
State Diagram	Shows how single object behaves across many use cases.
Use Case	Elicits requirements from users in meaningful chunks. Construction planning is built around delivering some use cases in each iteration. Basis for system testing.

Appendix B

Changes between UML Versions

When the first edition of this book appeared on the shelves, the UML was in version 1.0. Much of it appeared to have stabilized, and it was in the process of OMG recognition. Since then, there have been a number of revisions. In this appendix, I describe the significant changes that have occurred since 1.0 and how those changes affect the material in this book.

This appendix summarizes the changes so you can keep up to date if you have an earlier printing of the book. I have made changes to the book to keep up with the UML, so if you have a later printing, it describes the situation as it was as of the print date.

Revisions to the UML

The earliest public release of what came to be the UML was version 0.8 of the Unified Method. It was released for OOPSLA, which took place in October 1995. This was the work of Booch and Rumbaugh, as Jacobson did not join Rational until around that time. In 1996, Rational released versions 0.9 and 0.91, which included Jacobson's work. After the latter version, they changed the name to the UML.

Rational submitted version 1.0 of the UML to the OMG Analysis and Design Task Force in January 1997. Subsequently, Rational combined that version of the UML with other items and submitted a single proposal for the OMG standard in September 1997, for version 1.1 of the UML. This was adopted by the OMG toward the end of 1997. However, in a fit of darkest obfuscation, the OMG called this standard version 1.0. So, now the UML was both OMG version 1.0 and Rational version 1.1, not to be confused with Rational 1.0. In practice, everyone calls that standard version 1.1.

UML 1.1 had a number of minor visible changes from version 1.0.

In adopting UML 1.1, the OMG set up a Revision Task Force (RTF), chaired by Cris Kobryn, to tidy up various loose ends associated with the UML. The OMG released version 1.2 internally in July 1998. This release was internal in that 1.1 remained the official UML standard. You could think of version 1.2 as a beta release. In practice, this distinction hardly mattered, as the only changes in the standard were editorial: fixing typos, grammatical errors, and the like.

A more significant change occurred with version 1.3. Again, though, this is an internal release, so it is not an official OMG standard. However, the changes were more significant this time, most notably affecting use cases and activity diagrams. The amigos' *User Guide* and *Reference Manual* were published late in 1998; these books reflected the 1.3 changes before the official 1.3 documents were made public, which caused some confusion.

Scheduled Future Revisions

This is almost certainly out of date by the time you read this. For a more up-to-date picture, visit my Web site: **http://ourworld.compuserve.com/home-pages/martin_fowler**.

The 1.3 documents are now available for public comment. By April of 1999, the RTF submitted a revised UML to the OMG, which will be called version 1.4. The RTF expects that the only difference between 1.3 and 1.4 will involve polishing. Unless something very odd happens, the OMG will then adopt 1.4 as the new official standard some time in 1999. At that point, the OMG Analysis and Design Task Force will take over the UML and consider any future moves.

Changes in UML Distilled

As these revisions go on, I've been trying to keep up by revising *UML Distilled* with subsequent printings. I've also taken the opportunity to fix errors and make clarifications.

The first through fifth printings were based on UML 1.0. Any changes to the UML between these printings were minor. The sixth printing took UML 1.1 into account; however, due to a glitch, the inside covers still showed 1.0 notation.

The seventh through 10th printings were based on UML 1.2; the 11th printing was the first to use UML 1.3. Printings based on versions of the UML after 1.0 have the UML version number on the front cover. (Unfortunately, a printing error meant that some copies of the 10th printing were labeled as 1.3—I'm sorry about that.)

The first though sixth printings of the second edition were based on version 1.3. The seventh printing was the first to take into account the minor changes of version 1.4. I can't tell you what later printings will be based on without a crystal ball.

In the rest of this appendix, I'll summarize the two major changes in the UML, from 1.0 to 1.1 and from 1.2 to 1.3. I'll also summarize the minor changes from 1.3 to 1.4. I won't discuss all of the changes that occur, but rather only those that change something I said in *UML Distilled*, or that represent important features that I would have discussed in *UML Distilled*.

I am continuing to follow the spirit of *UML Distilled:* to discuss the key elements of UML as they affect the application of the UML within real-world projects. As ever, the selections and advice are my own. If there is any conflict between what I say and the official UML documents, the UML documents are the ones to follow. (But do let me know, so I can make corrections.)

I have also taken the opportunity to indicate any important errors and omissions in the earlier printings. Thanks to the readers who have pointed these out to me.

Changes from UML 1.0 to 1.1

Type and Implementation Class

In the first edition of *UML Distilled*, I talked about perspectives and how they altered the way people draw and interpret models—in particular, class diagrams. UML now takes this into account by saying that all classes on a class diagram can be specialized as either types or implementation classes.

An **implementation class** corresponds to a class in the software environment in which you are developing. A **type** is rather more nebulous; it represents a less implementation-bound abstraction. This could be a CORBA type, a specification perspective of a class, or a conceptual perspective. If necessary, you can add stereotypes to differentiate further.

You can state that for a particular diagram, all classes follow a particular stereotype. This is what you would do when drawing a diagram from a particular perspective. The implementation perspective would use implementation classes, whereas the specification and conceptual perspective would use types.

You use the realization relationship to indicate that an implementation class implements one or more types.

There is a distinction between type and interface. An interface is intended to directly correspond to a Java or COM style interface. Interfaces thus have only operations and no attributes.

You may use only single, static classification with implementation classes, but you can use multiple and dynamic classification with types. (I assume this is because the major OO languages follow single, static classification. If one fine day you use a language that supports multiple or dynamic classification, that restriction really should not apply.)

Complete and Incomplete Discriminator Constraints

In previous printings of *UML Distilled*, I said that the {complete} constraint on a generalization indicated that all instances of the supertype must also be an instance of a subtype within that partition. UML 1.1 defines instead that {complete} indicates that all subtypes within that partition have been specified, which is not quite the same thing. I have found some inconsistency on the interpretation of this constraint, so you should be wary of it. If you do want to indicate that all instances of the supertype should be an instance of one of the subtypes, I suggest using another constraint to avoid confusion. Currently, I am using {mandatory}.

Composition

In UML 1.0, using composition implied that the link was immutable (or frozen), at least for single-valued components. That constraint is no longer part of the definition.

Immutability and Frozen

UML defines the constraint {frozen} to define immutability on association roles. As it's currently defined, it doesn't seem to apply it to attributes or classes. In my practice, I now use the term frozen instead of immutability, and I'm happy to apply the constraint to association roles, classes, and attributes.

Returns on Sequence Diagrams

In UML 1.0, a return on a sequence diagram was distinguished by using a stick arrowhead instead of a solid arrowhead (see previous printings). This was something of a pain, since the distinction was too subtle and easy to miss. UML 1.1 uses a dashed arrow for a return, which pleases me, as it makes returns much more obvious. (Since I used dashed returns in *Analysis Patterns*, it also makes me look influential.) You can name what is returned for later use by using the form *enoughStock := check()*.

Use of the Term "Role"

In UML 1.0, the term **role** primarily indicated a direction on an association (see previous printings). UML 1.1 refers to this usage as an **association role**. There is also a **collaboration role**, which is a role that an instance of a class plays in a collaboration. UML 1.1 gives a lot more emphasis to collaborations, and it looks like this usage of "role" may become the primary one.

Changes from UML 1.2 (and 1.1) to 1.3 (and 1.4)

Use Cases

The changes to use cases involve new relationships between use cases.

UML 1.1 has two use case relationships: «uses» and «extends», both of which are stereotypes of generalization. UML 1.3 offers three relationships.

- The «include» construct is a stereotype of dependency. This indicates that the path of one use case is included in another. Typically, this occurs when a few use cases share common steps. The included use case can factor out the common behavior. An example from an ATM might be that Withdraw Money and Make Transfer both use Validate Customer. This replaces the common use of «uses».

- Use case **generalization** indicates that one use case is a variation on another. Thus, we might have one use case for Withdraw Money (the base use case) and a separate use case to handle the case when the withdrawal is refused due to lack of funds. The refusal could be handled as a use case that specializes the withdrawal use case. (You could also handle it as just another scenario within the Withdraw Money use case.) A specializing use case like this may change any aspect of the base use case.

- The «extend» construct is a stereotype of dependency. This provides a more controlled form of extension than the generalization relationship. Here the base use case declares a number of extension points. The extending use case can alter behavior only at those extension points. So, if you are buying a product on line, you might have a use case for buying a product with extension points for capturing the shipping information and capturing payment information. That use case could then be extended for a regular customer for which this information would be obtained in a different way.

There is some confusion about the relationship between the old relationships and the new ones.

Most people used «uses» the way the 1.3 «includes» is used, so for most people, we can say that «includes» replaces «uses». And most people used 1.1 «extends» in both the controlled manner of the 1.3 «extends» and as a general overriding in the style of the 1.3 generalization. So, you can think that 1.1 «extends» has been split into the 1.3 «extend» and generalization.

Now, although this explanation covers most usage of the UML that I've seen, it isn't the strictly correct way of using those old relationships. However, most people didn't follow the strict usage, and I don't really want to get into all that here.

Activity Diagrams

When the UML reached version 1.2, there were quite a few open questions about the semantics of activity diagrams. So, the 1.3 effort involved quite a lot of tightening up on these semantics.

For conditional behavior, you can now use the diamond-shaped decision activity for a merge of behavior as well as a branch. Although neither branches nor merges are necessary to describe conditional behavior, it is increasingly common style to show them so that you can bracket conditional behavior.

The synchronization bar is now referred to as a **fork** (when splitting control) or as a **join** (when synchronizing control together). However, you can no longer add arbitrary conditions to joins. Also, you must follow matching rules to ensure that forks and joins match up. Essentially, this means that each fork must have a corresponding join that joins the threads started by that fork. You can nest fork and joins, though, and you can eliminate forks and joins on the diagram when threads go directly form one fork to another fork (or one join to another join).

Joins are fired only when all incoming threads complete. However, you can have a condition on a thread coming out of a fork. If that condition is false, that thread is considered complete for joining purposes.

The multiple trigger feature is no longer present. In its place, you can have dynamic concurrency in an activity (shown with a * inside an activity box). Such an activity may be invoked several times in parallel; all of its invocations must complete before any outgoing transition can be taken. This is loosely equivalent to, although less flexible than, a multiple trigger and matching synchronization condition.

These rules reduce some of flexibility of activity diagrams, but they do ensure that activity diagrams are truly special cases of state machines. The relationship between activity diagrams and state machines was a matter of some debate in the RTF. Future versions of the UML (after 1.4) may well make activity diagrams a completely different form of diagram.

Changes from UML 1.3 to 1.4

The most visible change in UML 1.4 is the addition of profiles. A **profile** allows a group of extensions to be collected together into a coherent set. The UML documentation includes a couple of example profiles. Together with this, there's greater formalism involved in defining a stereotype, and model elements can now have multiple stereotypes (they were limited to one stereotype in UML 1.3).

Artifacts have also been added to the UML. An **artifact** is a physical manifestation of a component. For example, Xerces is a component, and all of those copies of the Xerces jar on my disk drive are artifacts that implement the Xerces component.

Prior to 1.3, there was nothing in the UML metamodel to handle Java's *package* visibility. Now there is; the symbol is ~.

Bibliography

Kent Beck: *Smalltalk Best Practice Patterns*. Prentice Hall, 1996.

Kent Beck: *Extreme Programming Explained: Embrace Change*. Addison-Wesley, 2000.

Kent Beck and Ward Cunningham: "A Laboratory for Teaching Object-Oriented Thinking." *Proceedings of OOPSLA 89*. SIGPLAN Notices, Vol. 24, No. 10, pp. 1–6. See <**http://c2.com/doc/oopsla89/paper.html**>.

Grady Booch: *Object-Oriented Analysis and Design with Applications, Second Edition*. Addison-Wesley, 1994.

Grady Booch: *Object Solutions: Managing the Object-Oriented Project*. Addison-Wesley, 1996.

Grady Booch, James Rumbaugh, and Ivar Jacobson [three amigos]: *The Unified Modeling Language User Guide*. Addison-Wesley, 1999.

Frank Buschmann, Regine Meunier, Hans Rohnert, Peter Sommerlad, and Michael Stal: *Pattern-Oriented Software Architecture: A System of Patterns*. John Wiley & Sons, 1996.

Peter Coad and Jill Nicola: *Object-Oriented Programming*. Yourdon, 1993.

Peter Coad and Edward Yourdon: *Object-Oriented Analysis*. Yourdon, 1991a.

Peter Coad and Edward Yourdon: *Object-Oriented Design*. Yourdon, 1991b.

Peter Coad, David North, and Mark Mayfield: *Object Models: Strategies, Patterns and Applications*. Prentice Hall, 1995.

Alistair Cockburn: *Surviving Object-Oriented Projects*. Addison-Wesley, 1998.

Alistair Cockburn: *Writing Effective Use Cases*. Addison-Wesley, 2001.

Larry Constantine and Lucy Lockwood: *Software for Use*. Addison-Wesley, 2000.

Steve Cook and John Daniels: *Designing Object Systems: Object-Oriented Modeling with Syntropy.* Prentice Hall, 1994.

James O. Coplien: "A Generative Development Process Pattern Language." In Coplien and Schmidt, 1995, pp. 183–237.

James O. Coplien and Douglas C. Schmidt, eds.: *Pattern Languages of Program Design* [PLoPD1]. Addison-Wesley, 1995.

Ward Cunningham: "EPISODES: A Pattern Language of Competitive Development." In Vlissides, Coplien, and Kerth, 1996, pp. 371–388.

Bruce Powel Douglass: *Real-Time UML.* Addison-Wesley, 1998.

Martin Fowler: *Analysis Patterns: Reusable Object Models.* Addison-Wesley, 1997.

Martin Fowler: *Refactoring: Improving the Design of Existing Programs.* Addison-Wesley, 1999.

Erich Gamma, Richard Helm, Ralph Johnson, and John Vlissides [Gang of Four]: *Design Patterns: Elements of Reusable Object-Oriented Software.* Addison-Wesley, 1995.

Adele Goldberg and Kenneth S. Rubin: *Succeeding with Objects: Decision Frameworks for Project Management.* Addison-Wesley, 1995.

David Harel: "Statecharts: A Visual Formalism for Complex Systems." In *Science of Computer Programming*, Vol. 8, 1987.

Ivar Jacobson, Grady Booch, and James Rumbaugh [three amigos]: *The Unified Software Development Process.* Addison-Wesley, 1999.

Ivar Jacobson, Magnus Christerson, Patrik Jonsson, and Gunnar Övergaard: *Object-Oriented Software Engineering: A Use Case Driven Approach.* Addison-Wesley, 1992.

Ivar Jacobson, Maria Ericsson, and Agneta Jacobson: *The Object Advantage: Business Process Reengineering with Object Technology.* Addison-Wesley, 1995.

Andrew Koenig and Barbara Moo: *Ruminations on C++: A Decade of Programming Insight and Experience.* Addison-Wesley, 1997.

Philippe Kruchten: *The Rational Unified Process: An Introduction.* Addison-Wesley, 1999.

Craig Larman: *Applying UML and Patterns*. Prentice Hall, 1998.

James Martin and James J. Odell: *Object-Oriented Methods: A Founda-tion (UML Edition)*. Prentice Hall, 1998.

Robert Cecil Martin: *Designing Object-Oriented C++ Applications: Using the Booch Method*. Prentice Hall, 1995.

Steve McConnell: *Rapid Development: Taming Wild Software Schedules*. Microsoft Press, 1996.

Steve McConnell: *Software Project Survival Guide*. Microsoft Press, 1998.

Bertrand Meyer: *Object-Oriented Software Construction*. Prentice Hall, 1997.

William F. Opdyke: "Refactoring Object-Oriented Frameworks." Ph.D. thesis, University of Illinois at Urbana-Champaign, 1992. See <**ftp:// st.cs.uiuc.edu/pub/papers/refactoring/opdyke-thesis.ps.Z**>.

Trygve Reenskaug: *Working with Objects*. Prentice Hall, 1996.

James Rumbaugh: *OMT Insights*. SIGS Books, 1996.

James Rumbaugh, Ivar Jacobson, and Grady Booch [three amigos]: *The Unified Modeling Language Reference Manual*. Addison-Wesley, 1999.

James Rumbaugh, Michael Blaha, William Premerlani, Frederick Eddy, and William Lorenzen: *Object-Oriented Modeling and Design*. Prentice Hall, 1991.

Geri Schneider and Jason P. Winters: *Applying Use Cases: A Practical Guide*. Addison-Wesley, 1998.

Sally Shlaer and Stephen J. Mellor: *Object-Oriented Systems Analysis: Modeling the World in Data*. Yourdon, 1989.

Sally Shlaer and Stephen J. Mellor: *Object Lifecycles: Modeling the World in States*. Yourdon, 1991.

Sally Shlaer and Stephen J. Mellor: "Recursive Design of an Applica-tion Independent Architecture." *IEEE Software*, Vol. 14, No. 1, 1997.

John M. Vlissides, James O. Coplien, and Norman L. Kerth, eds.: *Pattern Languages of Program Design 2* [PLoPD2]. Addison-Wesley, 1996.

Kim Walden and Jean-Marc Nerson: *Seamless Object-Oriented Software Architecture: Analysis and Design of Reliable Systems*. Prentice Hall, 1995.

Jos Warmer and Anneke Kleppe: *The Object Constraint Language: Precise Modeling with UML*. Addison-Wesley, 1998.

Rebecca Wirfs-Brock, Brian Wilkerson, and Lauren Wiener: *Designing Object-Oriented Software*. Prentice Hall, 1990.

Index

W

Y

The Unified Modeling Language User Guide

Grady Booch, James Rumbaugh, and Ivar Jacobson
Addison-Wesley Object Technology Series

The Unified Modeling Language User Guide is a two-color introduction to the core eighty percent of the Unified Modeling Language, approaching it in a layered fashion and showing the application of the UML to modeling problems across a wide variety of application domains. This landmark book is suitable for developers unfamiliar with the UML or modeling in general, and will also be useful to experienced developers who wish to learn how to apply the UML to advanced problems.

0-201-57168-4 • Hardcover • 512 pages • ©1999

Surviving Object-Oriented Projects

A Manager's Guide
Alistair Cockburn
Addison-Wesley Object Technology Series

This book allows you to survive and ultimately succeed with an object-oriented project. Alistair Cockburn draws on his personal experience and extensive knowledge to provide the information that managers need to combat the unforeseen challenges that await them during project implementation. Independent of language or programming environment, the book supports its key points through short case studies taken from real object-oriented projects, and an appendix collects these guidelines and solutions into brief "crib sheets"—ideal for handy reference.

0-201-49834-0 • Paperback •272 pages • ©1998

Objects, Components, and Frameworks with UML

The Catalysis[SM] Approach
Desmond Francis D'Souza and Alan Cameron Wills
Addison-Wesley Object Technology Series

Catalysis is a rapidly emerging UML-based method for component and framework-based development with objects. The authors describe a unique UML-based approach to precise specification of component interfaces using a type model, enabling precise external description of behavior without constraining implementations. This approach provides application developers and system architects with well-defined and reusable techniques that help them build open distributed object systems from components and frameworks.

0-201-31012-0 • Paperback • 816 pages • ©1999

Doing Hard Time

Developing Real-Time Systems with UML, Objects, Frameworks, and Patterns

Bruce Powel Douglass

Addison-Wesley Object Technology Series

Doing Hard Time is written to facilitate the daunting process of developing real-time systems. The author presents an embedded systems programming methodology that has been proven successful in practice. The process outlined in this book allows application developers to apply practical techniques—garnered from the mainstream areas of object-oriented software development—to meet the demanding qualifications of real-time programming.

0-201-49837-5 • Hardcover with CD-ROM • 800 pages • ©1999

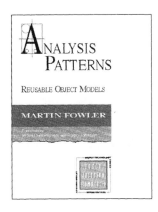

Analysis Patterns

Reusable Object Models

Martin Fowler

Addison-Wesley Object Technology Series

Martin Fowler shares with you his wealth of object modeling experience and his keen eye for solving repeating problems and transforming the solutions into reusable models. *Analysis Patterns* provides a catalog of patterns that have emerged in a wide range of domains, including trading, measurement, accounting, and organizational relationships.

0-201-89542-0 • Hardcover • 384 pages • ©1997

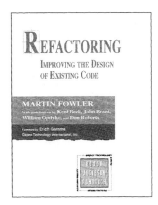

Refactoring

Improving the Design of Existing Code

Martin Fowler with contributions by Kent Beck, John Brant, William Opdyke, and Don Roberts

Addison-Wesley Object Technology Series

Refactoring is the process of changing a software system in such a way that it does not alter the external behavior of the code, yet improves its external structure. In this book, Martin Fowler et al. show you where opportunities for refactoring can typically be found, and how to go about reworking a bad design into a good one. In addition to discussing the various techniques of refactoring, the authors provide a detailed catalog of more than seventy proven refactorings.

0-201-48567-2 • Hardcover • 464 pages • ©1999

Software Reuse

Architecture, Process, and Organization for Business Success
Ivar Jacobson, Martin Griss, Patrik Jonsson
Addison-Wesley Object Technology Series

This book brings software engineers, designers, programmers, and their managers a giant step closer to a future in which object-oriented component-based software engineering is the norm. Jacobson, Griss, and Jonsson develop a coherent model and set of guidelines for ensuring success with large-scale, systematic, OO reuse. Their framework, referred to as "Reuse-Driven Software Engineering Business" (Reuse Business) deals systematically with the key business process, architecture, and organization issues that hinder success with reuse.

0-201-92476-5 • Hardcover • 528 pages • ©1997

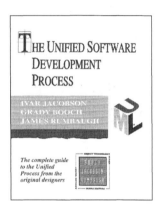

The Unified Software Development Process

Ivar Jacobson, Grady Booch, James Rumbaugh
Addison-Wesley Object Technology Series

The Unified Software Development Process goes beyond other object-oriented analysis and design methods by detailing a family of processes that incorporate the complete lifecycle of software development. This new book, representing the collaboration of Ivar Jacobson, Grady Booch, and James Rumbaugh, clearly describes the different higher-level constructs—notation as well as semantics—used in the models. Thus, stereotypes such as use cases and actors, packages, classes, interfaces, active classes, processes and threads, nodes, and most relations are described intuitively in the context of a model.

0-201-57169-2 • Hardcover • 512 pages • ©1999

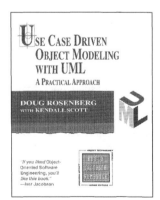

Use Case Driven Object Modeling with UML

A Practical Approach
Doug Rosenberg with Kendall Scott
Addison-Wesley Object Technology Series

This book presents a streamlined approach to UML modeling that includes a minimal but sufficient set of diagrams and techniques you can use to get from use cases to code quickly and efficiently. *Use Case Driven Object Modeling with UML* provides practical guidance that will allow software developers to produce UML models quickly and efficiently, while maintaining traceability from user requirements through detailed design and coding. The authors draw upon their extensive industry experience to present proven methods for driving the object modeling process forward from use cases in a simple and straightforward manner.

0-201-43289-7 • Paperback • 192 pages • ©1999

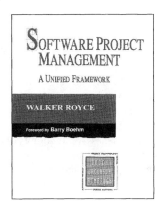

Software Project Management

A Unified Framework
Walker Royce
Foreword by Barry Boehm
Addison-Wesley Object Technology Series

This book presents a new management framework uniquely suited to the complexities of modern software development. Walker Royce's pragmatic perspective exposes the shortcomings of many well-accepted management priorities, and equips software professionals with state-of-the-art knowledge derived from his twenty years of successful from-the-trenches management experience. In short, the book provides the software industry with field-proven benchmarks for making tactical decisions and strategic choices that will enhance an organization's probability of success.

0-201-30958-0 • Hardcover • 448 pages • ©1998

The Unified Modeling Language Reference Manual

James Rumbaugh, Ivar Jacobson, Grady Booch
Addison-Wesley Object Technology Series

James Rumbaugh, Ivar Jacobson, and Grady Booch have created the definitive reference to the UML. This two-color book covers every aspect and detail of the UML and presents the modeling language in a useful reference format that serious software architects or programmers will need on their bookshelf. The book is organized by topic and designed for quick access. The authors also provide the necessary information to enable existing OMT, Booch, and OOSE notation users to make the transition to UML. The book provides an overview of the semantic foundation of the UML through a concise appendix.

0-201-30998-X • Hardcover with CD-ROM • 576 pages • ©1999

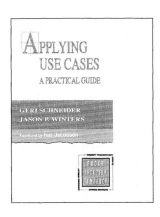

Applying Use Cases

A Practical Guide
Geri Schneider and Jason P. Winters
Addison-Wesley Object Technology Series

Applying Use Cases provides a practical and clear introduction to developing use cases, demonstrating their use via a continuing case study. Using the Unified Software Development Process as a framework and the Unified Modeling Language as a notation, the authors lead the reader through applying use cases in the different phases of the process, focusing on where and how use cases are best applied. The book also offers insight into the common mistakes and pitfalls that can plague an object-oriented project.

0-201-30981-5 • Paperback • 208 pages • ©1998

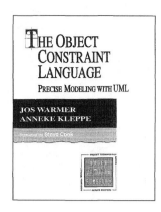

The Object Constraint Language
Precise Modeling with UML
Jos Warmer and Anneke Kleppe
Addison-Wesley Object Technology Series

The Object Constraint Language is a new notational language, a subset of
the Unified Modeling Language, that allows software developers to express
a set of rules that govern very specific aspects of an object in object-oriented
applications. With the OCL, developers are able to more easily express
unique limitations and write the fine print that is often necessary in complex
software designs. The authors' pragmatic approach and illustrative use
of examples will help application developers quickly get up to speed.

0-201-37940-6 • Paperback • 144 pages • ©1999